AF531116

MIRACLES AND METAPHORS

MÍRZÁ ABU'L-FAḌL GULPÁYGÁNÍ

Mírzá Abu'l-Faḍl Gulpáygání

MIRACLES AND METAPHORS

translated from the Arabic
and anotated
by

Juan Ricardo Cole

Kalimát Press
Los Angeles

First Edition

Originally published in 1900 in Cairo, Egypt,
as *ad-Durar al-Bahiyyah*

Manufactured in the United States of America

Library of Congress Cataloging in Publication Data

Gulpáyagání, Abú al-Faḍl, 1844–1914.
Miracles and metaphors.

Translation of: Durar al-bahíyah.
"Originally published in 1900 in Cairo, Egypt."
1. Bahaism—Doctrines. I. Cole, Juan Ricardo.
II. Title.
BP370.G813 297'.892 82-15309
ISBN 0-933770-22-7 AACR2

Translator's Dedication

To
Badí'u'lláh Faríd,
Háshim Farnúsh,
Kamálu'd-Dín Bakhtávar,
and all the other
intellectual and spiritual heirs
of Abu'l-Faḍl in our day
who so loved their blessed Faith
that they rushed
to the field of martyrdom
for its sake.

Their sublime thoughts once
enlightened us for a moment;
Their lofty example now
illumines us for all eternity.

Translator's Note

Bible verses are given according to the Revised Standard Version of the King James Bible. Qur'án verses are given according to the translation of A.J. Arberry, *The Koran Interpreted* (New York: Macmillan, 1973). However, I have sometimes modified the translation, either to bring out an aspect of the verse's meaning required by the context of the discussion, or to make the English more understandable. The numbering of the Qur'án verses is given according to the standard Egyptian numbering rather than the Western system used by Arberry.

Unless otherwise indicated, all annotations are the translator's.

My thanks to Shihábu'd-Dín Zahrá'í, through whose generosity I acquired a copy of Mírzá Abu'l-Faḍl's book, and from whom I learned a great deal about the latter's thought.

My thanks also to Bahia Faraju'lláh Gulick who kindly checked my translation against the original Arabic for accuracy, and to Anthony A. Lee who edited my English prose.

Contents

MÍRZÁ ABU'L-FAḌL (seated right)
with Ḥájí Mírzá Ḥaydar-'Alí (seated left) and other friends

Introduction

"BEFORE ATTAINING to the gift of faith, human beings are like the dead; and after attainment of faith, all achieve nothingness at the sacred threshold of the Divine." With these words Mírzá Abu'l-Faḍl used to turn aside every query about his life story. Speaking at a gathering of the friends on the day news of Abu'l-Faḍl's death reached Haifa, 'Abdu'l-Bahá said of him, "In all this time I never heard him use the word 'I'—'I said this' or 'I wrote that.'"

This scholar of towering intellect and prodigious erudition, who by any standard may well be considered the most learned man of the first century of the Bahá'í Era, was also a model of humility, detachment, service to the Cause, and servitude to his fellow-believers. So highly prized were these qualities by 'Abdu'l-Bahá, and so great was His love for Mírzá Abu'l-Faḍl, that once while in the United States, hearing of Abu'l-Faḍl's illness in Egypt, He sent the following cable to the friends in Cairo: "See to the comfort of Abu'l-Faḍá'il. He consists of my own self."

ABU'L-FAḌL WAS BORN in the town of Gulpáygán, in central Iran, in 1844, the very year of the declaration of the Báb. He came from a family of religious scholars, and he pursued the same path. He quickly distinguished himself at the local seminary and proceeded to an institution of higher religious learning in Isfahan. So brilliant was his record and reputation that before he was thirty he was installed as the master teacher of a prestigious seminary in Ṭihrán. In Isfahan he had come into contact with Bahá'ís; and in Ṭihrán he was pursued by some tenacious Bahá'í teachers whom he debated, ridiculed and rejected for nearly three years. The veils of intellectual pride and traditional learning which kept the light from reaching his heart were parted by a Bahá'í of humble rank and no schooling.

The story is charming and profoundly revealing, for it contains the key to Abu'l-Faḍl's turn of mind and to the thrust of his lifelong scholarly labors on behalf of the Faith of Bahá'u'lláh, of which the present volume is a representative example. One day as he waited at a roadside blacksmith shop for his donkey to be shod, the blacksmith said to him, "Mullá, I have heard of some holy traditions of the blessed imáms which I have difficulty understanding. Can you help me?"

Abu'l-Faḍl assented.

The blacksmith said, "I have heard the mullás quoting a holy tradition on the subject of God's mercy in sending down the rains: that every drop of rain is entrusted to an angel of God who brings it down to earth. Is this tradition true?"

Abu'l-Faḍl answered, "Yes."

"Again I have heard," the blacksmith went on, "on the subject of the ritual uncleanliness of dogs: there is a holy tradition that angels do not descend to houses where dogs are kept. Is this true?"

Again Abu'l-Faḍl answered affirmatively.

"Then," the blacksmith said, "we should see no rain fall onto houses which have dogs. How is it that the rains, when they come, come down everywhere?"

Abu'l-Faḍl was greatly perturbed by the man's conundrum, but his companions told him, "Never mind that troublemaker. He is just a misguided Bábí.'' For Abu'l-Faḍl, however, as he was to retell later in life, the dilemma epitomized the incongruence of sedulous, uncritical and literal acceptance of religious scriptures to enlightened faith and the gift of reason. The elaborate edifice of dogmatic knowledge which was his legacy and his pride could not stand the test of the common sense of an ordinary man. He then began a new course of serious and fair-minded study of the Writings of the Báb and Bahá'u'lláh. Before him were opening not just new visions of spiritual reality, but also new ways of looking at truth, and the pursuit of truth. In the end, it was the force of the *Kitáb-i Íqán* that confirmed him. That book was to remain a beacon throughout his life. Much of what he later wrote and said as a Bahá'í rests on the premises of the *Íqán*: that is, the striving for a spiritually valid and reaffirming understanding of the Scriptures which is also compatible with the human intellect. The year was 1876.

The next ten years were spent in traveling and teaching throughout Iran at the behest of Bahá'u'lláh. He was imprisoned several times for his faith, and on some occasions he was in danger of being put to death. His own family turned against him and deprived him of his rightful patrimony. It was through Varqá, the poet, martyr-to-be, that he received encouragement from Bahá'u'lláh to devote his pen as well as his tongue to the furtherance of the Faith and to utilize his scholarship for its defense. In 1886, he left Persia for 'Ishqábád, Russia, at Bahá'u'lláh's request. Within two months of his arrival in that city, he was to witness the momentous events surrounding the martyrdom of one of the Bahá'ís (Ḥájí Muḥammad Riḍá Iṣfahání), and serve as the chief Bahá'í spokesman at the historic trial of the murders, which resulted in recognition of the independent character of the Bahá'í community in Russian Turkistan.

FROM 'ISHQÁBÁD Abu'l-Faḍl went to Samarqand and Bukhara. These cities had been at the zenith of Islamic civilization in Central Asia, vibrant centers of intellectual activity, eight centuries earlier. The decay in which he found them, combined with his lack of apparent success at direct teaching in those parts, coinciding with the news of the passing of Bahá'u'lláh, left him in a mood of relative quiet and inactivity.

Out of this torpor, he was called by 'Abdu'l-Bahá to the Holy Land in 1894. His spirit was galvanized. He was launched on the most productive and significant labors of his life. The twenty years that were left to him until his death in 1914 were filled with teaching, traveling and writing—always at the direction of his beloved Master. His first assignment was to proceed to Egypt.

AT THE TURN OF THE CENTURY, Egypt was the hub of what was left of a once dynamic Muslim civilization. Centuries-long traditions of religious scholarship, represented by the venerable institution of al-Azhar, the school of higher Islamic learning, were being animated by the winds of "reform" and "modernism." 'Abdu'l-Bahá wanted to inject the relevance of the Bahá'í Faith into that atmosphere, and Mírzá Abu'l-Faḍl was His chosen instrument. He wisely advised him to adopt an indirect approach. For had Abu'l-Faḍl attempted to talk openly about the Faith from the outset, he would never have received a respectful hearing in the intellectual circles of Cairo. In the eyes of conservative Sunní scholars, a Persian "apostate" from Shí'í Islam would have had a double mark against him. Instead, he gained his entry into those circles by the judicious demonstration of his remarkable intellect and his brilliant grasp of comparative religious history and thought. He was particularly noted for his original turn of mind in interpretation of religious scriptures. Soon he had a large and avid circle of al-Azhar students and other devotees who were gradually introduced to the Faith. A significantly large number of them ultimately became Bahá'ís.

In Cairo, Mírzá Abu'l-Faḍl became a magnet of Bahá'í intellectual activity. From Persia and India, Turkistan and Caucasus, Syria and the Holy Land, even from Burma and China Bahá'ís corresponded with him—many of them referred to him by 'Abdu'l-Bahá—raising questions of scriptural interpretation. Objections to and attacks on the Faith were sent to him for response and defense.

With the publication of some of his writings in Egypt, the phase of indirect teaching and guarded identity came to an end. In 1898, *Falá'id*, his eloquent response to an attack on the Faith by a certain Muslim cleric from the Caucasus, was published in Cairo. Since it was written in Persian, it did not attract much attention or opposition in Arabic-speaking Egypt. In 1900, Shaykh Faraj'ulláh Zakí al-Kurdí, one of the devoted group of Abu'l-Faḍl's al-Azhar disciples who had become a Bahá'í, published the original of the present collection of essays in Arabic under the title *ad-Durar al-Bahiyyah* (The brilliant pearls).

Mírzá Abu'l-Faḍl now emerged in Egypt as the learned exponent of the Cause of Bahá'u'lláh. His erudition in Islamic sciences and his brilliant defense of Islam against tendentious missionaries and orientalists elicited the admiration of open-minded people, and his unconcealed identity as a Bahá'í aroused the vilification and abuse of dogmatic religious fundamentalists.

FROM THIS VORTEX of activity and public attention 'Abdu'l-Bahá lifted Mírzá Abu'l-Faḍl into yet another arena of crucial service to the Cause. The nascent community of Bahá'ís in America was in dire need of an authoritative and coherent understanding of the fundamentals of its Faith. Above all, it needed a devoted and persuasive expounder of the theme of the Covenant if it was to achieve the essential unity that was the prerequisite for its growth. In December of 1900, 'Abdu'l-Bahá sent Laura Clifford Barney to Egypt to accompany Abu'l-Faḍl to the West. After a three month stay with the Bahá'ís in Paris, he sailed for America. 'Abdu'l-Bahá sent a young man, Ali-Kuli Khan, to translate for him because Mírzá Abu'l-Faḍl knew no English. He remained in America just a few months short of four years. He held regular classes for the Bahá'ís and for seekers in Washington, New York, Chicago, and Boston.

His classes at Green Acre left an indelible mark on the young and eager community. It was here, in an atmosphere fostered by Sarah Farmer, that the ghost of Emerson blended with talk of Nirvana and Spiritualism. Here, where professors of philosophy from Harvard and Columbia mingled with artists and men and women of affluence and influence, the figure of this disciplined and almost ascetic man towered above all. The wealth of his knowledge, the rigor of his intellect, the range of his awareness of the currents of philosophic and scientific thought in the West, and the originality of his approach to traditional subjects were

MÍRZÁ ABU'L-FAḌL (center) AT GREEN ACRE
with Ahamid Saraf (l.) and Ali-Kuli Khan (r.)

MÍRZÁ ABU'L-FAḌL (center) AND FRIENDS
Taken the day he left America to return to the Holy Land.

sources of amazement and enlightenment to all whose paths he crossed.

It may be said without exaggeration that it was Mírzá Abu'l-Faḍl who prepared the ground for the visit of his beloved Master to America. While in this country he wrote *The Bahá'í Proofs* which was published in Ali-Kuli Khan's English translation. This was his contribution to the teaching of the Cause in a predominantly Christian society.

The vital and tender bonds of love and devotion that were forged between this scholar of the East and the young community of American Bahá'ís whom he had helped deepen in the Covenant of Bahá'u'lláh were touchingly evident on the day they gathered to bid him farewell on 29 November 1904. In a rare reference to his own life he said: "My tongue falters at offering adequate thanks to God for having granted me such loving brothers and sisters. I am reminded of a passage in the Gospels [Mark 10:29–30]: 'And Jesus answered and said, "Verily I say unto you, there is no man that hath left house, or brethren, or sisters, or father, or mother, or wife, or children, or lands, for my sake, and the gospel's, but that he shall receive a hundredfold now in this time . . ."' Praised be God that in this glorious age all the verses of the Holy Books have come to pass.

"Thirty-two years ago when I was leaving my hometown, I was still a Muslim, and my mother, sister and brothers gathered to say good-bye to me. Three years later when I entered this Mighty Cause in Ṭihrán, all my relatives abandoned me and left me friendless, helpless and alone in the world. Now consider the bounty and generosity of our Master who has fulfilled His promise and granted me hundreds of times over what was lost in His path. . . . How can I ever adequately thank the Divine Bounties for having bestowed upon me such spiritual kin as you?''

THE LAST TEN YEARS of Mírzá Abu'l-Faḍl's life were spent in Cairo, with occasional sojourns in Beirut and visits to Haifa. During the time that 'Abdu'l-Bahá was in Alexandria, in 1910, He rented a house nearby for Abu'l-Faḍl so that he could be near Him. Grown frail and in ill health, this solitary man was busy with his research and writing to the end of his days. Numerous treatises on the history of the Bahá'í Faith, the Covenant of Bahá'u'lláh, the proofs and prophecies of the Qur'án and of the Bible, belong to these last years.

He died January 21, 1914, in Cairo. He was designated a Hand of the Cause; and his remains are buried now in the Cairo Bahá'í cemetery next to another Hand of the Cause of God, Lua Gettsinger, with whom he shares a joint monument. He was named Muḥammad, and Abu'l-Faḍl, Father of Excellence, was his given apellation. But 'Abdu'l-Bahá always addressed him as Abu'l-Faḍá'il (the plural form), Father of All Excellences.

THE PRESENT COLLECTION of essays published together first in 1900, is fairly representative of Abu'l-Faḍl's pattern of scholarship. The impetus is provided by questions put to him by Bahá'ís and others, often dealing with difficulties arising from literal interpretation of Holy Scriptures. Refutation of attacks upon the integrity of the Bahá'í Revelation, defense of the rightful place of Islam in the progressive history of religions, issues of proof and verification in comparative religious history, constitute the major themes of these essays. Among the questioners are such Muslim learned men as Shaykh Núru'd-Dín of

Sind, who apparently corresponded with Mírzá Abu'l-Faḍl from Karachi, and who went on to become the second titular head of the Ahmadiyya movement in India; and Ḥusayn Effendi Rúhí, a longtime Bahá'í companion of Abu'l-Faḍl.

What is remarkable about the nature of Abu'l-Faḍl's responses is that they are firmly based upon meticulous and prodigious historical inquiry and encyclopedic knowledge of sources, aided by full and free use of deductive reasoning. In other words, he combines the best—and vast—advantages of his traditional knowledge with an open, critical and questioning mind. He characterizes the intellectual bankruptcy of the traditional curricula of the Islamic schools as the "mouldering repetitions of the elders."

Above all, it is the aim of his scholarship that informs and infuses the quality and the methodology of his works. That aim is, at all times, the affirmation of the Cause of God and the furtherance of its teachings. In pursuit of that aim Abu'l-Faḍl acquired a rare balance of devotion, humility and love of learning. He was convinced that with the aid of prayer most problems of religious, and even scientific, enquiry may be solved or understood. As he points out in one of the essays of this volume, knowledge is nothing but comprehension of the reality of things, and the reality of things can only be reflected in hearts which are pure. That purity is attainable through prayer and spiritual concentration.

THERE IS VALUE for the modern reader in these essays, not only in the historical interest of the subject matters, but in Abu'l-Faḍl's aims and methods of dealing with them. The seriousness of religious scholarship and the integrity of scriptural knowledge may not be as prevalent as they were in Abu'l-Faḍl's time, but a far more debased and intellectually repugnant version of these, in the form of a simplistic and simple-minded fundamentalism, is resurgent everywhere in our time. Abu'l-Faḍl's gifts of enlightened faith, profound knowledge and judicious reasoning are examples to the rising generation of Baha'í scholars who must cope with it.

JUAN COLE's excellent translation and annotation of these essays is cause for hope that the "extended family" of the spiritual kin of Mírzá Abu'l-Faḍá'il, the Father of All Excellences, is growing.

Amin Banani
Santa Monica
February 1982

MIRACLES AND METAPHORS

MÍRZÁ ABU'L-FAḌL GULPÁYGÁNÍ

Invocation

In the Name of God, the Merciful, the Compassionate.

I render praise and thanksgiving to our Lord, the Exalted, the Most High. I prostrate myself before His Countenance, the Most Holy, the Glorious, the Most Glorious. I ask blessings and peace for the Dawning-Places of His light, the Fountainheads of His Manifestation among His creatures—especially the noble Branch that has come forth from the Ancient Root, the true Mystery that has emanated from the will of his Lord, the Merciful, the Compassionate. May God cause us to be among those that seek the protection of his banner, and count us among his chosen and beloved ones.

The Lord has restored the glory of the ancients, and
Raised up for splendor an imperishable palace.
It still stands at the towering heights: that which once
Enraptured the breeze in the knolls of the gardens.

I, Abu'l-Faḍl Muḥammad Gulpáygání of Iran, the son of Muḥammad-Riḍá, testify that the eminent and erudite Indian scholar Núru'd-Dín (may God illumine both of us with the light of certitude) asked me some scholarly religious questions. Some of these were related to matters of ancient history. Anyone with awareness will see that this is difficult terrain to cover and that these matters are shrouded in mystery. For this era is of great antiquity: all traces of it have been destroyed, and its light has faded. We, therefore, have chosen to respond to him according to our limited knowledge and understanding, keeping the discussion concise.

We confess the fewness of our wares and our lack of any qualification to compete in this arena. We beseech God at the very beginning of this discussion to safeguard us by His grace from errors in our views and our discourse. He, verily, is our Guardian in the beginning and in the end.

Part I

Answers to Questions of an Indian Scholar

NOAH'S ARK

Attributed to Miskin. Indian Painting (Mughal), c. 1590. Possibly from the Diwan of Hafiz. Courtesy of the Freer Gallery of Art, Smithsonian Institution, Washington, D.C.

The First Question

Question: S͟hayk͟h Núru'd-Dín al-Hindí asked our belief concerning Noah's age. Did he live 950 years as revealed in the Holy Qur'án, or does this have another meaning?

Answer: Those who are knowledgeable concerning such matters are divided between two views, one religious and the other scientific.

The religious view is as follows: It is well known that whoever believes in the truth of the mission of the Prophet Muḥammad, and believes that the Holy Qur'án is the Book of God revealed from heaven, necessarily accepts the validity of everything contained in that noble book. He acknowledges the truth of whatever was revealed therein, whether or not it accords with the understanding of the people, as long as clear reason does not judge it impossible and no decisive proof against it can be shown to exist.

Anyone who has the least familiarity with rational proofs and logical analogies accepts as self-evident that the only objection to the extreme longevity the ancients are said to have enjoyed is that such a thing is simply unlikely. However, in reality it is not rationally untenable. For not the least convincing proof exists that it is impossible for people to enjoy a greater longevity than is normal in our own times. This is especially so for human beings who lived in ancient times and past ages because there is no way to investigate their circumstances or the length of their lives, owing to the inaccessibility of their history and the disappearance of all traces of their civilization. A prudent mind will refrain from deciding against that which was revealed in the Holy Qur'án merely because it is unlikely. "It is verily a decisive word, nor is it in jest."[1]

As for the scientific view, it is this: It is obvious that no scholarly investigator will accept the authority of any statements unless he can determine their original sources and the degree to which these are reliable and trustworthy. It is, moveover, well known that there are only four historical traditions containing information on how the creation began which are held in high esteem by great nations and whose sources they find dependable. These are Buddhist history (that of the Chinese), Hindu history (that of the original inhabitants of India), Zoroastrian history (that of the first peoples of Persia and their great rulers), and Hebrew history (that of the Jews and others who accept the mission of Moses). These historical traditions differ irreconcilably in their concepts, contain the diverse beliefs of their peoples, exhibit a huge variance in chronology, and clearly differ as to the names and events they mention. In spite of all this, the observer will note with amazement that these historical traditions accord with one another in two ways. One is their common assertion that the ancients lived extremely long lives compared to what became normal in later times, and the other is their intermixture with stories greatly resembling myths (in the eyes of scholarly investigators), or riddles, enigmas, and symbols (in the eyes of moderates).

As for the Buddhist, Hindu, and Zoroastrian histories, they contain no mention of Adam and Eve, or of

Seth, Noah, or the others. Neither do they mention their stories or the events associated with their lives. Not even similar names occur in them. Only the Hebrew history mentions these names, and from there they were transmitted to the Christians and Muslims.

The Prophet Muḥammad said, "We, the concourse of Prophets, were sent to address people according to the capacity of their minds." And likewise, "Speak to the people of that with which they are familiar; do you wish God and His Messenger to be called liars?" Thus was it related by the learned judge Averroes of Spain in his book *Exposition on Methods of Evidence Concerning the Doctrines of the Muslim Community*, citing al-Bukhárí.[2] Therefore, given this situation, it is impermissible for the scholarly investigator to depend on the verses of the Qur'án and the traditions of the Prophet in historical questions.

It is clear that the prophets and Manifestations of the Cause of God were sent to guide the nations, to improve their characters, and to bring the people nearer to their Source and ultimate Goal. They were not sent as historians, astronomers, philosophers, or natural scientists. Their position in the world of creation is like that of the heart in the body: it has a universal position with a general effect. The position of the learned in the world of earthly dominion is like that of a specific organ. That is, they have a particular position and a special effect. Therefore, the prophets have indulged the people in regard to their historical notions, folk stories, and scientific principles, and have spoken to them according to these. They conversed as was appropriate to their audience and hid certain realities behind the curtain of allusion. They secluded the holy maidens of meaning in the palaces of sacred verses, veiling them in eloquent metaphors.

A rational human being will therefore have no doubt that those things mentioned in the Holy Qur'án, such as how the creation commenced, the debate of the angels, the stories of Adam, of Satan, and of Noah and the flood, are all realities. These speak of repeated promises to renew the world and refer to the appointed times for the expiration (through the advent of the primal Holy Reality and the renewal of the divine laws) of the terms allotted to the nations. But, from the point of view of science, it is impermissible for the historian to depend on the literal meaning of these verses. This is because he cannot discount the very real possibility that they possess a higher significance and are subject to sublime, figurative interpretations which differ from the understanding that might be gained from their external sense.

The possibility that these verses should be interpreted figuratively is hardly a remote one, nor is it an unlikely concept which can be disregarded by the eminent and learned as insignificant. For it has been revealed in the Holy Qur'án, "Nay, they deny that which their knowledge does not encompass, though its interpretation has not yet come to them."[3] Another verse says, "Do they look for aught else but its interpretation? The day its interpretation comes, those who forgot it before shall say, 'Indeed, our Lord's Messengers came with the truth.'"[4] Moreover, the traditions and practice of the Prophet have genuinely established and made it abundantly clear that the verses of the Qur'án have mysterious and profound esoteric meanings and exalted, subtle, figurative interpretations. These are known by those who have dedicated themselves to the Holy Book and are intimately familiar with it, for God has granted to His steadfast and sincere servants the ability to discover them.

By figurative interpretation is meant only the original meanings intended, which God veiled in the inner depths of the verses and hid behind a curtain of metaphors. Such interpretation is not something for mere mortals, nor should every ignorant one plunge haphazardly into it, nor every obscure scholar interpret the verses according to his opinion. Some of the ignorant have done this in their pride, and have gone astray and led many others astray with their interpretations. They have thus kept people from the wellspring of life, the path of salvation. Rather, this is a matter for the Manifestations of the Cause of God, the Vindicators of His promise. This has been said clearly in the Qur'án: "So when We recite it, follow thou its recitation. Then Ours it is to explain it."[5]

It has, therefore, been established that the historian cannot depend on the outward meaning of the verses of the Qur'án for historical knowledge, and that Noah and his like are not mentioned in the rest of the ancient histories. And so, the historian is left with only the Pentateuch and the other books of the Old Testament. If he avoids sectarian prejudices, blind traditionalism, and popular fabrications, an insightful critic will perceive that these holy books have two distinct sorts of teachings, which deserve further attention.

The first sort is the teachings attributed to God, which are spoken by God, or which consist of revelation from God. These contain ordinances, commandments, laws, and directions. They also contain warnings and glad tidings—the most important of which are predictions concerning the signs, portents, and circumstances signaling the advent of the Day of God. Such are the Ten Commandments of Moses and his hymn of blessing at the end of Deuteronomy, the

Psalms of David, the book of Isaiah the Prophet, and the books of Jeremiah, Daniel, Ezekiel, Zechariah, and other prophets of Israel. Anyone upon whom God has bestowed insight and the gift of knowledge can distinguish between human words and the verses of God, and will confess that all these books are made up of divine verses and heavenly prophecies and warnings. These shine forth from the blessed Bush of Moses like a lighted lamp in the depths of night, or a star rising in the farthest heaven.

The second sort of teachings is those that contain information concerning such historical matters as how the creation began, the development of various tribes, the dispersal of mankind over the earth, the history of the lives and times of the prophets, and the enumeration of kings and the events occurring during their reigns. Of this sort are the histories contained in the Pentateuch, from the beginning of Adam's creation until the death of Moses. Likewise included are the historical books of Joshua, Judges, Samuel I and II, Kings I and II, Chronicles I and II, Ezra, Nehemiah, and so on. In these works there is no open statement, or any sign, or indeed the faintest hint that they are celestial revelation or divine inspiration or speech. Therefore, it is impermissible for the historian to depend on them, or to assert that their contents contain no error, or to consider them revelation. This could be done only if one were sure of the identity of the authors of these books. Anyone who is aware of the degree to which scholars differ over the identities of the writers of these histories, and the evidence on which each faction depends in establishing its view or belief, knows that to rely on the correctness of the contents of these books is not permissible. It would be utterly foolish for a person of critical reason to depend on a book whose author cannot be established by research, or to consider it divine revelation when, in spite of extensive examination and detailed investigation, its author and source remain unknown.

For example, when one pages through the works of the most eminent scholars on the identity of the author of the Pentateuch, which is the foundation of the Old Testament and the basis of Hebrew history, one sees that there are great differences, which no one could hope to resolve through inquiry and investigation. Nor could one expect to arrive at a foundation that is, in the final analysis, at all sound. Many scholars used to think that Moses was the author of these books. However, the final passages of this book refute those scholars and render their views worthless, as they mention the death of Moses and how the Israelites held a wake for him. Other pieces of evidence clearly indicate the books were composed long after Moses' passing. Some scholars have, without any evidence, asserted that everything but the last two chapters of Deuteronomy was written by Moses, and that these latter are the work of Joshua, the son of Nun. He is said to have written them and added them to the five books of Moses to complete it by finishing Moses' biography and clarifying the circumstances of the people after his death. Others say that these books were composed by Jeremiah or another of the prophets of Israel. This assertion, like the preceding ones, suffers from weak justification and lack of evidence.

One group of scholars has said (and perhaps correctly so, since the argument has some force) that they are compositions of Ezra the soothsayer, referred to in the Qur'án as Uzayr.[6] After the people returned from the Babylonian exile at the order of Ardi<u>sh</u>ír the Great, Jerusalem was rebuilt, the Jews were gathered together, and the House of David was revived. At that time, the people asked Ezra for a copy of the Hebrew

Bible. He was a learned man, a skillful writer, and a pious soothsayer. He had studied in the great schools of the city of Babylon, acquiring wide knowledge and useful arts unrivaled for his time. Babylon was then the refuge of civilization and the dawning-place of the light of science and philosophy. Ezra then wrote, in answer to the people's request, five books on how the creation began, how the people split up, how the tribes branched off, and how mankind developed until the death of Moses. He included therein the story of the revelation given to Moses by his Lord and of how Moses (or Joshua, according to some of the Bible's verses: see Joshua 24) legislated for the organization of his people's affairs.

To sum up: first, it is apparent that the stories of Noah and the others are not mentioned in the histories of the great peoples of antiquity, such as the Chinese, the Persians, and the Indians. At the same time, no one can belittle the breadth of their knowledge, the antiquity of their civilizations, the remoteness of their eras, the vastness of their kingdoms, or the wide fame of their attainments. Second, research is unable to establish the identity of the author of the Hebrew Pentateuch. Finally, it is well known that neither the Prophet Muḥammad nor the rest of the prophets ever engaged in disputes with the people about their historical beliefs, but addressed them according to their local traditions. It is therefore necessary to conclude that interpreters and investigators may not come to a final opinion on these matters on the basis of sure knowledge. If the way should be barred to individual judgment, then only the religious point of view would remain, and this would consist of worshipful submission to the literal meaning of whatever has issued from the prophets and messengers.

One of the most astounding things is that, so far, researchers have failed to find in the ancient Egyptian ruins even the slightest evidence that the Israelites were ever in Egypt. This has confused the scholars, attracted the attention of the wise and intelligent, thrown suspicion on what used to be considered universally accepted, and forced historians to reexamine and carefully investigate even those things they had considered self-evident. No trace has been found of Moses' mission to the Israelites, their plea for salvation from Pharaoh's tyranny through Moses' leadership, or their emigration to the plains of Syria under his standard. Yet the Israelites were a warlike people, numbering the warriors among them at eight hundred thousand or more. Pharaoh pursued them with his troops, who all drowned in the sea of their infidelity and atheism.

In the ancient Egyptian ruins, as scholars are aware, accurate histories have been discovered which time had obscured and buried so that their mention had been obliterated from the history books. Centuries and cycles passed, until God revived them in this glorious age. This is the age wherein mysteries have been unraveled, the light of lights has dawned, and the accumulated darkness of confusion has been unexpectedly dispelled. A number of Western scholars have arisen and have discovered the truth of Egyptian history from ancient ruins. From these have appeared the names of the kings and pharaohs, their deeds and circumstances, the number of their houses and families, their religion and customs, and their gods and rites.

These ruins have allowed scholars to recover clear references to the pharaohs, to order the sequence of their reigns correctly, to enrich history with a new epoch, and to give the science [of archeology] a firm foundation. All these ancient artifacts, including the mummified corpses of the pharaohs, are preserved in the Egyptian Museum. Travelers and learned men set out for their great temples, coming from Europe and America to uncover historical information and to visit the Egyptian monuments.

They have not yet found any corroboration for the Old Testament stories about Moses, Aaron, and Joshua, or their circumstances. Neither have they found anything concerning their forebears, such as Adam, Seth, and Noah. Those who believe in the Old Testament histories are bewildered as to how to fill in this huge gap. They have been profoundly alarmed by the crumbling of the foundations of this great historical tradition. For it is unimaginable that the Egyptians, who depicted on walls every event, great or small, and inscribed in stone everything that happened in Egypt, whether temporal or religious in nature, should have neglected to mention such extraordinary and stupendous occurrences as Moses' demonstration of amazing signs and the drowning of Pharaoh and his huge army.

Some have propped their chins in the palms of their hands in astonishment, still hoping for some way to adjust things or patch them up. Others are waiting for more investigation and research so that they may find a path to corroboration and agreement. God knows best how this affair of the archeologists and those who are waiting expectantly will end up. In any case, this should suffice those with insight.

The Second Question

QUESTION: He asked (may God preserve him) about the meaning of the angels' argument with God concerning His appointment of Adam as His vicegerent on earth.*

ANSWER: May God confirm both of us by His spirit and bestow His mercy upon us. Know, my erudite friend, that this matter is intimately connected with the question of knowing that there are pure spirits and celestial souls, and understanding that these are essentially sanctified above matter and that they require matter in order to act.

First it must be recognized that philosophers and researchers in the scholarly community have defined "spirit" in different ways. The best, most perfect, and clearest of these is that spirit is an abstract substance separate from matter in essence but not in act. It will not be hidden from the wise that this definition, insofar as it is a definition by negation, fails to elucidate the reality of the essence of the thing described. It is a comprehensive, restrictive definition which, nonetheless, better explains the intent of the word "spirit" than other definitions. It can be known from this definition, for instance, that spirit is different from matter

*Qur'án 2:30: "And when thy Lord said to the angels, 'I am setting upon the earth a viceroy.' They said, 'What, wilt Thou set therein one who will do corruption there, and shed blood, while we proclaim Thy praise and called Thee Holy?' He said, 'Assuredly I know what you know not.'" See also Qur'án 38:71–88.

and material things in regard to its essence. Spirit cannot be described by such attributes as ingress and egress, independence and inherence, advance and retreat, movement and stillness. Eyes cannot perceive it, nor can the other senses. Yet it remains in need of matter in all acts, and inseparable from it in all conditions, for it is unimaginable that matter be stripped from it.

No act can issue from spirit except through matter, and it is inconceivable that an effect could be produced by spirit save through the instrumentality of matter. For instance, it is impossible to imagine that the acts of seeing, hearing, writing, or thinking could proceed from spirit alone, except through the instrumentality of the eye, the ear, the hand, the brain, and so on. In this respect there is no difference between holy celestial spirits, rational human spirits, perceptive animal spirits, or base satanic spirits. These are all terms and experessions referring to actions, attributes, and properties rather than to the common abstract nature of their essence and their need for matter in order to act.

Many have remained heedless of this point, and ancients and moderns have both wandered astray in this desert. To this the holy verses have referred: "And had we made him an angel, we would have made him [in the form of] a man, and we would have thus confused them concerning the very thing about which they are sowing confusion."* Those lost in the wasteland of delusion, heedless of the true meaning of that which the All-Possessing, the All-Knowing had prom-

*Qur'án 6:9. The Qur'án here points out to the Meccans that they would not have been able to recognize an angel, as he would be sent down so as to resemble an ordinary man.

ised, saw in the heavenly scriptures (particularly the Holy Gospel) that the Lord Messenger (or the Lord who would descend) would come with a company of favored angels and a host of the Concourse on High, and that he would be rendered victorious by a multitude of swooping angels and those riding behind.[7] But when the noble messenger Muḥammad appeared—may the blessings and peace of God be upon him and upon his House—they saw a simple man who ate food, strolled in the market, kept company with other Arabs, and sat upon the ground. There were neither angels hovering over his head nor hosts of those imagined spirits walking before and behind him. They criticized Muḥammad for failing to fulfill the Revelation because he did not meet an unreasonable condition.

They clamored, shouted, elaborated, and expatiated at length. "And they said, 'What is wrong with this messenger, that he eats food and walks in the markets? Why has an angel not been sent down to him, to be a warner with him?'"[8] The previously cited verse was revealed to reproach and to silence these people, to refute their proofs, and to rebut their fancies. It informed them that there is no effulgence of the spirit save in the form of a human being and that angels only descend in such a form.

To put it more clearly, pure substance can only have an effect through the instrumentality of bodies. An angel who descends is nothing other than a human being. What is the meaning of *human being*? He is the supreme talisman; the most noble substance; the form created for unchallenged dominion over all the world; the perfect, distinguished reality; the first revealed sign; the essence receptive of all forms, high and low.

All these names and attributes refer to the human being, and all else is fancy, dream, illusion, and imagination.

How often have philosophers attempted to establish that there exists an absolutely pure intellect separate from matter both in essence and in act! However, the steed of their argument has stumbled on their evidence, the blade of their investigation has failed to strike home, and the standard of their proof has been hauled down. They spoke with great bombast and verbosity, but in the end produced nothing. How could it be otherwise? For this idea is simply a relic of the idle notions of the pagans and the daydreams of the Greeks, left over from a time when the veils of doubt obscured the truth on all sides and the gloom of the blackest night enveloped all regions. Among the peculiar properties of night is that nothing can be seen except prostrate souls drowning in slumber and minds lost in a labyrinth of dreams. The great scholar Naṣíru'd-Dín Ṭúsí, may God sanctify his soul, put this consisely and eloquently in his book, the *Tajríd,* wherein he demonstrated the weakness of their proofs. He said, "As for the [universal] intellect, there is no evidence of its impossibility, but the evidence for its existence is weak."[9] However, I say that even as the evidence for the existence of the metaphysical intellects is held to be weak by Ṭúsí, so also the evidence for the possibility of a being which is sanctified from matter both in essence and in act is unconvincing as far as those of mature thought are concerned.*

Let us leave off this plunge into the black depths

*Medieval Neoplatonic Muslim philosophers, in discussing metaphysics and the creation of the world, argued for a series of descending emanations from God. The first of these was the intellect, from which emanated the universal soul, from which in turn of idle thoughts and return to the exposition of the solution we were proposing to this question. Those endued with intelligence know that God in His consummate wisdom and all-encompassing power created two opposing forces, two conflicting spirits. The first is the sanctified spirit, which does good and emanates compassion, inspiring propriety and wisdom. The prophets have called it Gabriel, the Holy Spirit, or the Faithful Spirit. The philosophers have termed it the Celestial Spirit, the Universal Intellect, the First Emanation, and the Heavenly Soul. The second is the wicked spirit, which does evil and provokes rancor, inspiring sin and error. The prophets have referred to it as Satan, the devil; and in the Holy Gospel as the Beast and the Behemoth. The philosophers have called it the base spirit and the absolute self.

It has been established that the relationship between spirits and bodies is only that of connection and encompassment, not that of infusion and incarnation,

emanated universal form, from which finally emanated universal matter. And so the cosmos came into being. One of the arguments these Neoplatonists employed was that only intellect could act without matter; soul and form need matter to accomplish anything. Thus, only the universal intellect could begin the chain of actions, or emanations, which led to the creation of the world. The intellect, therefore, had to be the first emanation from God, and the source of all other emanations.

The eminent Shí'í thinker Ṭúsí (1201–1274 A.D.) does not deny the existence of the universal intellect here but finds the evidence for it to be weak. Abu'l-Faḍl denies that even universal intellect can act without matter, agreeing with Ṭúsí that this argument of the Neoplatonists is defective. However, Abu'-Faḍl and the Bahá'í Writings affirm on other grounds the existence of the universal intellect as the "first" or primary emanation from God. See 'Abdu'l-Bahá, *Some Answered Questions,* trans. Laura Clifford Barney (Wilmette, Ill.: Bahá'í Publishing Trust, rev. ed., 1981), p. 203.

Since in Bahá'í thought both matter and the universal intellect have always existed, the latter has never had to act without the instrumentality of matter.

or of entering and withdrawing. It has been shown that the mirrors reflecting the effulgences of the Holy Spirit are the hearts of the prophets and messengers, the innermost being of the Manifestations of the Cause of God, the Lord of the worlds. Their noble bodies are thrones upon which God is seated, temples for the worship of God, lamps shining with the light of God, manifestations of all His names and attributes, and instruments of His emanations and signs. In the same way, evil hearts are the seats of base spirits and vile selves, and are mirrors reflecting idle fancies and contemptible, delusive thoughts. Their bodies are instruments of error and manifestations of tests and divisions. Their tongues are the dragomans of Satan, and they are themselves the essence of the Evil One and enemies of the All-Merciful. But the hosts of Satan are the vanquished, and the armies of God are the victors.

If all this be recognized, the meaning of "angel" and "demon" will necessarily be understood, as will the meaning of the argument between God and the Concourse on High. It will also be seen that everything contained in the Holy Qur'án in this regard is only a statement of what has occurred, and what will happen, at the time of the appearance of the Manifestations of the Cause of God: the renewal of the world through their appearance; the return of the primal realities through their dawning; and the realization of the "Creation," the "Resurrection," the "Assembling," and the "Dispersal" through their Word. At such times the angel is distinguished from the demon, and the hosts of unbelief are weeded from the ranks of the army of God. Then will the good be known from the despicable, the base from the excellent, the lean from the fat, the denizens of hell from the inmates of heaven.

It is recognized and established among those of pure heart and illumined vision that the dispute among the Concourse on High only took place after God decided to set up a vicegerent upon the earth, to ordain a guardian, to prescribe the succession of the Branch which came forth from the Ancient Root, and to order that all should prostrate themselves before his noble countenance. Since the recurrence always resembles the original, God proclaimed that this dispute would be renewed. He preordained the occurrence of such opposition in the verse, "Say: it is the Great Announcement, to which ye are opposed. I had no knowledge of the Concourse on High when they quarreled."[10] God has stated openly in His Holy Book, with the greatest eloquence and the most lucid explanation, that enmity will inevitably break out among the Concourse on High, and a dispute is expected in the most high paradise. This is so that the people of the right hand will be distinguished from the people of the left hand, that the people of guidance might be told from those gone astray, the angel known from the demon, and the followers of Satan separated from the worshipers of the All-Merciful.

However, God commanded His Prophet to conceal the explanation of this quarreling and disputation, and to avoid giving the believers its details, leaving it general in its symbolism. Since God did this out of mercy toward His creation owing to their weakness, no doubt the erudite questioner will pardon us if we have spoken concisely and left this matter, after a profitable investigation, still somewhat ambiguous.

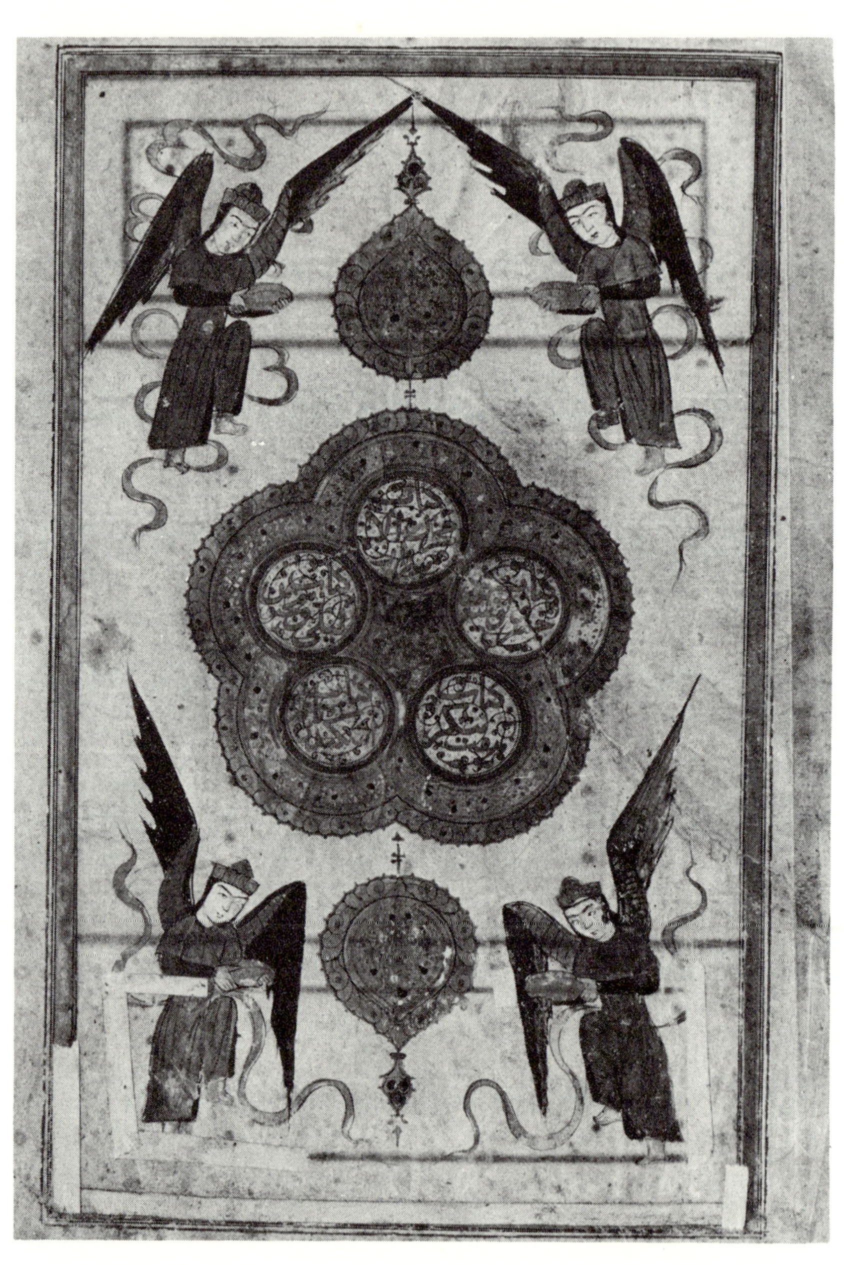

FOUR ANGELS
on the title page of the Khamsah by Nizami. Persian painting, 1450. The Metropolitan Museum of Art, Gift of Alexander Smith Cochran, 1913. [13.228.3]

The Third Question

QUESTION: He asked whether prayer, religious donations, fasting, and pilgrimage have real benefits and useful effect, or whether they are merely primitive pastimes and useless religious customs.

ANSWER: O eminent scholar! may God confirm us both with penetrating vision and sound views. Know that such matters depend on the belief that there is a true, wise, encompassing, and omnipotent God above His servants, and that this God sends messengers and prophets to establish divine laws and to found religions. It is unimaginable that anyone could embrace any of the religions without submitting to this truth, or that any reasonable person would bear the difficulties and discomforts of worship and service without recognizing this abstruse reality. We Bahá'ís believe that all religions were ordained by God, that they spread by His power, became exalted by His Word, and that they conquered the world through His will and volition.

Just as religions depend on recognition of the existence of God, they are also dependent on belief in the immortality of souls and their survival after separation from the body. Were it not for an acceptance of this truth, no reasonable person would ever embrace any religion or follow any divine law. Spirits are eternal, and the worlds of God are imperishable. Moreover, as we explained earlier, bodies are in need of spirits, and no act can appear from any faculty save by the instrumentality of souls. Spirits make manifest the acts that proceed from these faculties. Spirits conform to the attributes that are grounded in these faculties. Given all this, no thinking individual will doubt that religion cannot be complete unless it is based on two separate sorts of laws and founded on two firm foundations.

The first sort of law concerns the outward aspects of the world and the unity of nations. This includes the promulgation of justice and beneficence, the preservation of the rights of the people, and the establishment of manners involved in human relations and the best means of associating together. Moreover, it includes the ruling of subjects, the progress of nations, and other means whereby human society is preserved. It is upon this sort of law that the pillars of culture and civilization are reared.

The second type of law concerns the progress of souls, the purification of hearts, the refinement of characters, and the perfection of minds for the sake of their hoped-for survival in the worlds to come. This includes fasting, prayer, the mention and magnification of God, and other varieties of worship. It is obvious that some laws and ordinances were ordained for their spiritual properties and their benefit in the next life alone, such as prayers and the praise of God. These practices bear no relationship to any benefit to civilization or to the preservation of human society, except perhaps in some trivial respects. But there are also ordained laws concerning the externals of this world, which have no link with anything spiritual, such as most of the ordinances about politics and social and economic intercourse.

There are, moreover, those laws which were ordained because they possess both sorts of benefit discussed above, and these have splendid effects on both levels. They encourage good works including justice, beneficence, pilgrimage, charitable contributions, truthfulness, trustworthiness, purity, and cleanliness, and command the avoidance of evil deeds such as murder, adultery, lying, treachery, tyranny, calumny, slander, and so on. The adherence to good and the avoidance of evil have manifest effects, for thereby human beings progress, improve their characters, safeguard society, and protect the rights of the community.

An understanding of the way in which spirit is the actor and the effective agent (the body being nothing but an instrument) will necessarily lead us to an appreciation of the degree of the spirit's influence. For it is the spirit that performs the above-mentioned deeds and takes on virtuous or base characteristics. Character is only an attribute which inheres in the actor through the repetition of the act until it becomes a characteristic. It is on the basis of attributes that mankind will be gathered together on the Judgment Day, and it is by these attributes that the extent of our gain or loss shall be known.

Let us now discuss the benefits of the four ordinances about which the esteemed questioner has asked. May God guide him to the presence of His Name, the Self-Subsistent, and give him to drink of the sealed Wine.

As for prayer, it is a ladder for the believer, a solace to the eye of one possessed of certitude, a station of intimacy with God, and a place to attain the presence of God and to turn in repentence to Him. Prayer is humility before God, recognition of His lordship, affirmation of His unity, obedience to His will, and compliance with His every wish. Prayer thus has an effect on the spirit and makes the heart tender, removing it far from all cruelty and darkness. The heart then becomes aware of the virtues of servitude and perceives the full meaning of the rancor and evil caused by disobedience. Through prayer a human being will see the effect of things with illumined insight and understand the influence of his actions with perspicuous certainty. Beyond all this, he will even recognize that there is an omnipotent, all-encompassing, victorious, and almighty God Who visits retribution upon His servants for every offense, small or large, holding them responsible for every sin and crime. Such a one will necessarily strive to avoid transgressions and shameful acts, out of real apprehension and deep fear. This is the secret of the verses, "Prayer forbids indecency and dishonor," and "Seek you help in patience and prayer, for grievous it is, save to the humble."[11]

By the life of God! If prayers and other forms of worship did no more than bequeath certainty, and bestow detachment and assurance in regard to religion, this would be sufficient as a virtue. For there is no life save through religion and no religion except through certitude. Understand then the verse, "Serve thy Lord until certitude comes to thee."[12]

The reason certitude derives from worship is that certitude is the spirit's perception. The spirit is a perceptive faculty which encompasses the essences of all things, or on which their forms are imprinted. The spirit grows ever stronger and purer through worship. Moreover, whenever the worshiper is engaged in prayer—concentrating upon the meaning of its words and basic elements, feeling the ecstasy of being so engaged—he will be kept from the grave transgressions and offenses whereby the heart is hardened and the spirit is clouded.

When the power, clarity, and purity of the spirit grow, so too does the faculty of perceiving realities and their forms. The strong, purified spirit perceives the realities of things as they are through encompassing them. But the sullied spirit perceives the forms of things only through evidence and proof. Therefore, the sciences of the prophets are marked by direct perception, while the knowledge of the learned is obtained through analogy and evidence. Only those who have attained the station of certitude can know the full extent of this difference. Those who have not yet reached this station may deduce this difference from the writings of both sides. On the one hand are the prophets and the first generation of the people of faith; and on the other, the philosophers and the learned, who are masters of evidence and demonstration. The seeker will find between the writings of the two sides a clear distinction and a huge distance, as we shall, God willing, elucidate. This is only one of the signs of certitude, but it will suffice for those with insight.

No consideration should be given to the assertions of the partisans of naturalism—including materialists and Darwinists—who claim that the prophetic writings are only the products of fanciful emotions and hysterical imaginations—that they have no reality but have simply taken root in peoples' minds through long habituation and fervent study. For a man's progress through the stages of faith to the point where he will gladly give his life to protect his religion gives clear evidence for the soundness of his faith and the reality of his certitude. This transcendent quality—this astonishing attribute—is realized only through beliefs that require the exercise of independent judgment and the acquisition of knowledge, not through inherited beliefs which demand blind imitation. The difference between these two kinds of faith manifests itself as the first grows and spreads its influence, like healthy seed in good ground, while the second falls and fails, like rotten seed on barren earth.

It is obvious that matters concerning discernment and belief—such as doubt and certainty, opinion and decisive judgment, and so forth—are not things the outward senses can perceive. Geometrical proofs and philosophical analogies cannot be used to demonstrate them. Rather, it is deeds that give evidence of them and hearts that bear witness to them. This is the secret of the noble Qur'án verse wherein God addresses the Jews: "O Jews: if you assert that you are friends of God above all others, then long for death if you speak truly!"[13] The Jews believed they were the sacred people, the children of righteousness, the good and pure family, and the friends of God above all others. God silenced them with this proof and expelled them from the people of faith by explaining what was meant by "friends of God" and making the station of the lovers of God clear. It is established and certain among the people of insight that the doubter will be distinguished from the one possessed of certitude only when the storms of trials blow, when the cyclones of tests arise, when with sharp teeth and claws the rapacious predator attacks the unarmed believer, and when violent death bares its fangs. Then will the one who exercises independent judgment be known from the blind imitator, the steadfast from the feckless, and truth from falsehood.

We have, in our own time, seen a great many pure souls with courageous and immaculate hearts who, at the gathering of these storms and at thunderous tempests, poured out their lifeblood with the utmost joy. For the love of God, they counted their blood as worthless. They disdained life and welcomed death with the greatest ardor. They hastened to the field of sacrifice and hurried to the scene of their death with their faces exultant and their hearts full of cheer, so that everyone was bewildered at their forbearance, and every onlooker was astonished at their calm and steady mien. They did not recant their religion, nor did they conceal their belief. By the life of God, this is that real martyrdom which attests to the soundness of their religion and the reality of their certitude!

An even better proof of the loftiness of their certitude and the exalted station of their religion is their power to transform the hearts of others, their ability to exchange corrupt creeds for sound beliefs and to change repulsive, savage natures into good and pleasing ones. By them, God has curbed the wicked and perverse morals, and the evil customs and beliefs that were firmly established among the ancient peoples, as no philosopher ever could, even with all the power of his thought and the depth of his knowledge.

For God has granted to His chosen ones the capacity to convey His Word, to spread His religion, to establish His Cause, and to make manifest His proofs without drawing upon earthly, human forces. These chosen ones support themselves with nothing save divine power. They do not rely on acquired sciences or knowledge, on wealth or riches, on royal authority or sovereign power, or on kinship solidarity or cooperation.[14] They exalt the name of God's religion with brilliant divine power and need not raise it upon those outward pillars. This is a truth the recognition of which distinguishes the people of ignorance from the people of faith, and the people of doubt from the people of certitude.

Anyone who meditates upon the conditions of the first generation among the faithful, the companions of the prophets and messengers, such as the apostles of

Jesus or the companions of Muḥammad, will be able to perceive some of the signs of this mighty force and understand the meaning of this divine power. The disciples of Jesus promulgated the religion of God and transformed the absurd beliefs held by the nations. They abolished long-held savage customs of peoples around the world without distributing printed books or dazzling them with wondrous manufactured goods or opening schools of science or resorting to military force. They had no help from the thunderous rumbling of cannons, nor were they reinforced by the clatter of steel, on which modern men have depended and whereby they have become victorious. Rather, they spread the religion of God by their faith, erased unbelief by the power of their certitude, aided the Cause of God with their blood, and exalted His Word by offering up their lives. But the Jewish rabbis, the Zoroastrian priests, the philosophers of Greece, and the sages of Rome were unable to abolish even one of those absurd beliefs and customs, which seem so laughable today to their descendants and at which their successors and grandchildren scoff.

In the same way, the companions of the Prophet dispelled the gloom of unbelief from the world by the light of this celestial force and rooted out polytheism with this divine power. In order to perceive some of the effects of this mighty bestowal, it suffices to consider what is recorded in the noble biographies of the Prophet and in the authentic traditions from him. The great ones among the Prophet's Helpers*—when they believed in and accepted the Prophet in the last year prior to the emigration from Mecca to Medina—

*The Helpers (Anṣár) were the Medinans who became Muslims. They invited Muḥammad to take refuge from his enemies by emigrating from Mecca to their own nearby city.

requested that he dispatch one of his companions to them to instruct them in prayers and religious practices, and to call the people of Medina to Islam. He sent Muṣ'ab ibn 'Umayr, among others. Muṣ'ab was a mere youth, wholly ignorant of reading and writing. He was known for neither his eloquence nor his oratory and had only memorized the obligatory prayer and some verses of the Qur'án. He called the people of Medina to the new Faith, and through him the majority of Yat͟hrib's* inhabitants embraced Islam before the Prophet arrived there and before he unsheathed his sword—contrary to the claims of those who hold him in contempt.

Likewise, in our own time we have witnessed that some illiterates upon whom God bestowed this dazzling power have, with the potency of their certitude and the sincerity of their conviction, vanquished the hearts of ancient peoples who were wandering in the darkness of idle fancy and in the desert of blind imitation. They have transformed their inherited false dogmas into sound, demonstrable beliefs, destroyed their superstitions, and perfected their faith. Their ethics were renewed, their tastes edified, their vision set ablaze, and their consciences set at ease. Through the light of faith, their ignorance was turned into knowledge, their weakness into power, their treachery into trustworthiness, their evil into chastity, their estrangement into affection, their cowardice into valor, and their brutality into meekness.

In sum, all their old corrupt ways were transformed into new and virtuous morals, and their inbred deluded creeds were changed into sound and valid beliefs. Thus, any fair-minded person can judge their

*Yat͟hrib is another name for Medina.

transformation of character, their rebirth and renewal, in spite of their former lifelessness. All these things are but the effects of certitude; and certitude itself is a result of worship, as it was revealed to the trustworthy Prophet: "Serve thy Lord until certitude come to thee."[15] Therein is what will suffice those with insight.

As for religious donations, this is a matter the benefits of which shine forth brilliantly. Contributing to the Faith has a direct effect on the soul insofar as it develops within it the virtue of munificence while effacing the rancor caused by stinginess and avarice. Such contributions hold the key to generosity and well-being, which make command and leadership possible. For it is impossible to safeguard human society unless subjects pay a prescribed tax to their ruler so that he may spend it on the various means of protecting their rights, directing their affairs, improving their conditions, and exercising leadership over the general public. For the sake of all these benefits, God established such contributions as one of the primary ordinances of the Islamic religion and in the Qur'án clarified how they are to be spent. However, the people misconstrued the Word of God and corrupted the divine laws, spending these donations in ways God never commanded.* Therefore has their power become weakness, their life death, and their independence bondage. Thy Lord does not wrong His servants.

As for fasting, its effects are even more clear and manifest, more perfect and exalted. For fasting possesses all the benefits of prayer, which we have mentioned and elucidated, while it also effectively disciplines the animal self and curbs the defiance of

*Most fail to give such contributions, and the few who do so do not give them to the proper authorities.—Abu'l-Faḍl

the appetitive faculties.* This is obvious for all to see, and it does not require lengthy discourse or excessive explanation. For it is evident that man is one of the animal species, and animal faculties are intrinsically attracted to the natures imprinted on them and incline to the pleasures derived from their disposition. We have explained in our other works that the legislative faculty,† be it divine or human, belongs to the natural faculties and regulates the deeds that issue from the lower self. For it is impossible to restrain the willfulness of the self and turn it away from base pleasures and destructive, animal desires save by training it with the discipline of the Divine Law which has been handed down, and withholding it from grave offenses by means of prescribed moral standards. This should not be through arduous, artificial restraint, as the Sufis believe, or solely through refinement and learning in schools, as naturalist philosophers maintain.

As for pilgrimage, this is the most perfect commandment, encompassing both spiritual and civilizational benefits, both religious and worldly rule. For God has ordained therein rituals and acts of prayer, commemoration, and praise, which are useful for spiritual progress, as we have explained. Therein are also rules and practices which lead to mutual acquaintance, cooperation, association, and contact between various nations and races, and which offer great benefit to civilization.

If this blessed and praiseworthy act of pilgrimage

*One system of Platonic thought maintains that man has three natural faculties: the appetitive faculty (the source of all animal drives), the irascible faculty (the source of strong emotions), and the intellective faculty (the source of rational thought).

†That is, the legislative faculty is the human ability to make laws that govern society, whether this ability be exercised under the influence of divine revelation or of human reason.

involved no more abstruse effect or no greater deed (which any wise or astute person recognizes) than to provide a means for creating intimacy and harmony, unity and concord, among the great peoples—which we mentioned above—this would suffice to require that it be held in high regard, and recognized for its mighty effects. For it is not an easy matter to bring together each year—from the borders of China in the east to the farthest reaches of Africa in the west, and from the principalities of India in the south to the hinterlands of Siberia in the north—every person who is able, from the nobles of tribes and the leaders of nations, in this vast gathering, for the purpose of performing this great and arduous rite such that they see this as a religious duty and a divine command.

By the life of God, if the rulers of Islam and the caliphs and the kings who have taken possession of this Blessed Spot,* this noble land, knew how to make use of this lofty wisdom and divine policy, and if they treated the visitors of that Sacred House† in the best way—showing them the most fitting courtesy, facilitating their travel, preparing the means for their comfort—and if they arose to invite them to agreement and to warn them of the consequences of disunity, and alerted them to the benefits of harmony—then would they be able to establish a consensus among the Muslims and cause all the believers to stand beneath the shade of a single banner. Then would they acquire an invincible power and an exalted Word. But only the intelligent and pure esteem these things, while the obscure and the foolish hold them in

*Mecca.

†A reference to the Kaaba, the sacred cubelike building in Mecca which Muslims circumambulate during the pilgrimage, and toward which they pray each day.

disdain. And so, alas, they have not appreciated the value of this laudable wisdom and have not perceived the purpose of this apposite policy. They have mistreated the visitors to the ancient House, and robbed and plundered the pilgrims to that distant land, until the Dispensation of the Book* was ended and the sun of grace and glory set. Therein are signs for possessors of discernment.

*The Qur'án.

MOSES AND AARON

conjuring up a serpent from Moses' staff which attacks the Pharaoh's magicians. From Qisas al-Anbiya (History of the Prophets) of Nis͟hapurí, c. 1590–1600. Bibliothèque Nationale, Paris.

The Fourth Question

QUESTION: He asked (may God protect him) concerning the meaning intended by the staff of Moses and its ability to part the sea and make springs flow from rocks, as well as concerning the meaning of the miracles of Jesus and the meaning of the water that flowed from the Prophet's fingertips, as is related in the traditions.

ANSWER: May God grant you the joy of ascending to high stations and sublime goals! Know, illustrious scholar, that for all their exalted, lofty, and elevated station, the holy scriptures and prophetic sayings remain words, expressions, and designations. They therefore contain both literal, outward meanings and hidden, spiritual metaphors. In the same way, the hearts to which these words were revealed and the tongues that spoke these verses, though they were the thrones of divinity and the interpreters of heaven, remained human hearts and human tongues.

To put the matter more clearly: there is no doubt that the prophets to whom the books were revealed were human beings like all other men and spoke in the same way that other human beings speak. They expressed what was revealed to them in the same way that others express their own consciences. It is not rationally untenable that some of these expressions contain metaphors and figures of speech, metonymies, and similes. In the same way, it is possible for them to contain plain statements empty of allusion, and literal propositions not subject to figurative interpretation.

Many of the learned have taken the statements in the traditions literally and have thought that the staff actually turned into a serpent and that water really flowed from the fingers of the Lord of Prophets,* and have believed other amazing stories and miracles. On the other hand, a great many eminent scholars, who are knights in the arena of knowledge, have held that all such incidents reported in the holy books and traditions are figures of speech standing for rational matters and realities which sound reason will accept and healthy discrimination does not reject. They have therefore interpreted the staff as God's command and decree. Moses, with this staff, defeated Pharaoh and his troops and escaped the snares of pride and unbelief. With this staff, he struck the twelve tribes so that their hardened hearts grew tender, their constricted breasts were soothed, and their darkened bosoms were illumined. From these hearts the waters of knowledge and wisdom flowed, and the springs of grace and mercy burst forth. The Israelites then became sovereign rulers and great leaders, whereas before they were ignorant shepherds and lowly slaves upon whom the pharaohs imposed the worst scourge, and to whom they gave to drink of the bitterest dregs. They had stolen their daughters for their service, killed their sons, and enslaved their men. In the course of these tribulations, and in suffering these adversities, the Israelites became like motionless rocks and lifeless bodies. They found no refuge from their ordeals and no remedy for their maladies.

Then Moses appeared, and God gave him the

*Muḥammad.

power of legislation and prophecy and commanded him to deliver the children of Israel from the shame of their bondage and slavery. Two splendid consequences, which no knowledgeable person will deny, nor any man of insight ignore, followed upon this command (which was spoken of as a "staff") and this mission (which was called "the white hand").* First, all of Pharaoh's schemes and plots were undone. Second, Moses' people were redeemed from their broken condition, rescued from the degradation of captivity, and seated upon the throne of supreme authority.

And so, from these hardened hearts, which were like barren rocks, the springs of knowledge and wisdom gushed forth. Their religion became known to all mankind, and, over a period of fifteen hundred years, every tribe learned of their faith and their path. Then their dispensation expired and their era reached its end. They grew disunited in their speech, their ties were broken, their hearts grew hard and died, and the leprosy of degradation ate at their limbs and countenances. They went from the oppression of pharaohs to the tyranny of caesars, from slavery to the Egyptians to bondage under the Romans. At that point, the Sun of Reality dawned from the horizon of God's world, and the melodies of the Gospel rang out. God restored life to some among the people through the breath of Jesus. With his blessed hand he purified all the leprous faces and created the Christian religion. By this Faith he cleansed all of Europe of the decay of idol worship.

Then the years passed and the centuries followed one on another until the Sun of Guidance shone again from Arabia. The noble Prophet arose to establish the

*See Exod. 4:6–7. God changed Moses' hand to a leprous white and then returned it to normal, as a sign of his power.

Islamic Faith, and God caused springs of knowledge and divine wisdom to flow from his blessed fingers. The branches of guidance put forth their foliage, came into flower, and then gave fruit in the kingdoms of the East. The East and the West were thus prepared to attain equilibrium, to achieve their perfection, and to witness the descent of the Promised Lord from the clouds of glory. Thus, cycles revolved and ages expired until day dawned again and the Light of lights shone forth. The gloom of darkest night was dispelled from all regions. The Cause is God's, the One, the All-Conquering.

We Bahá'ís believe that the Manifestations of the Cause of God and the Repositories of His Revelation are, in reality, the manifestations of all His names and attributes, and the Dawning-Places for His verses and sayings. Not a single one of God's attributes becomes manifest on this primary plane save from them, and it is impossible to establish any of the exalted characteristics of glory or beauty save by them. Moreover, reason cannot accept that we can ascribe to the Essence of God any personal pronoun or any other allusion regarding the performance of any act, except if these refer to the Manifestations.

For the Divine Essence and the Supreme Reality is transcendent in its quintessence, exalted above description in its substance, and purified from attributes in its inmost being. Minds cannot discern it, nor can understanding attain to it. Consciousness cannot contain it, and the sense cannot encompass it. It cannot be described, named, or indicated. It cannot be specified by ascribing any pronoun to it, for the basis of all such ascription is sense perception, while it is beyond apprehension. It is clear that whatever is perceived is encompassed, and whatever is encompassed is limited. Whatever is limited has position, and this is an attribute of bodies and bodily things, above which all abstract things are exalted—how much more the Divine Essence, the Illumined Reality!

All that whereby God's essence is described, and everything which is added to and rests upon God—including such attributes as glory, grandeur, power, might, knowledge, wisdom, will, volition, and so on—refer, in reality, to the Manifestations of His Cause, the Dawning-Points of His light, the Repositories of His Revelation, and the Fountainheads of His theophany. This matter has been inscribed upon the Tablets of our most glorious Lord by the Pen of the Most High with detailed elucidations, and God has made manifest the essence of His mysteries in the scriptures that His sweet utterance has purified.

Since it has been established that the Manifestations of the Cause of God are the manifestations of God's power, might, will, and volition, then it follows that it is not impossible for them to perform miracles, to cause things to appear which others find impossible, because of the universality of that holy Soul which is effulgent in them. How could it be otherwise? They are mighty in their powers. They are the Spirit of God descended from heaven, and the Reality exalted above all things that subdues all beings and vanquishes all that is in the realms of the visible and invisible. Just as things appear from human beings which do not appear from other species of animals, owing to the universality of the human spirit in relation to the particularity of animal spirits, in the same way the prophets can produce things other cannot because of the universality of their spirit, the all-encompassing nature of their power, and the greatness of their might. In the same way that the wondrous deeds and glorious works manifested by human beings are miraculous for other species of animal—and, indeed, must be considered altogether impossible for the animals, in relation to their own powers—so the prophets manifest things that are miraculous for other human beings.

By the Life of God! Were those with penetrating insight to meditate upon the glad tidings and dire warnings proclaimed by the prophets and messengers concerning the cycles their people must pass through, their future progress, their halt, and then their decline —including prophecies of the period they would survive, specification of their allotted terms, and of what they would undergo as a result of their good and evil deeds—they would perceive the meaning of this Spirit's universality and the all-encompassing nature of its power. For the divine scriptures are the true heavenly repast.[16] They contain whatever souls hunger for—that whereby breasts are gladdened, eyes are delighted, and hearts are overjoyed.

Look, for instance, at the second Epistle of the Apostle Peter, who is known among the Arabs as Simon the Pure. He was the first to believe in the Spirit of God, Jesus, who descended from the heavens, and was his vice-regent over his servants after his ascension to the Concourse on High. This chosen apostle, this preferred leader, foretold in this epistle the future condition of the Christian community and the events which would befall the Christian peoples. But human minds cannot perceive such things even with all their lofty scientific understanding, or with their precise political foresight, or even with their sublime, yet merely human, acumen. Rather, this is a matter of celestial revelation and divine inspiration, which we have referred to as the encompassing of the soul and the universality of the Holy Spirit. Were it not for lack of space, and the fact that my mind is distracted by all the work I have to do, and the opposition of base enemies, I would have given a commentary on this noble epistle for those with clear vision. Thus might they witness the wondrous marvels God has reposited in the Book, for the understanding of which He has specialized those with acute minds.

Likewise, the glorious Qur'án reports the future condition of the Islamic nation in meticulous detail, until the end comes with the promised Theophany. It appoints the time of that Theophany, its place of origin, and the way in which his Cause will spread and his call will be promulgated. For instance, anyone who contemplates the holy verse, "And listen thou for the day when the caller shall call from a near place. On the day they hear the cry in truth, that is the day of coming forth,"[17] will see that it specifies the place where the Promised One will descend and predicts clearly that the call of the Lord will be raised from the Holy Land, which is the region nearest to Arabia. It is the western part of greater Syria, which lies near Jabal al-Quds, on the coast of the Mediterranean Sea between Asia and Europe. This place is the snow-white Holy Land, the redolent, illumined Spot. It is the scene of the Presence, the Point of Adoration for the pure ones, the homeland of the prophets, and the place from which the call of God is raised up between heaven and earth.

It is well known that Syria and the coastlands of the Mediterranean are vast realms containing famous lands and numerous cities, villages, and farms; and the Prophet himself explained that the Promised One would appear in the city of 'Akká, and that the repository of that light would be the celebrated plain of those regions. He lauded and extolled that city and its environs, mentioning its springs and wells in his holy sayings. He foretold for its inhabitants and visitors the greatest good, saying, "Blessed is he who hath seen 'Akká." This noble tradition became so widely known that specialists in language, like the author of the *Ṣiḥáḥ* and others, seized upon it and cited it in their books so that it has become a proverb.[18] Poets were so enamored of it that they used it in their poetry. Thus, in this tradition, and in many others like it which are recorded in the books of traditions, the Prophet set forth the details of all the blessed verses we mentioned above, elucidated them in the best possible manner, and firmly indicated where the Theophany would take place. He spoke most clearly.

The great ones among the learned have taken this tradition as a source for the details of their own prophecies and have referred to it in their speaches, essays, books, and other works. These include the Prince of the Believers, 'Alí ibn Abí Ṭálib, who was among the first believers; the great spiritual leader Ibnu'l-'Arabí; S͟hayk͟h Kamálu'd-Dín Muḥammad ibn Ṭalḥah; Sayyid as͟h-S͟ha'rání; and many others in later times.[19] Among the sayings as͟h-S͟h'rání quoted from the exalted traditions in his book *Sapphires and Jewels* (in the sixty-fifth discussion) is the Prophet's saying, "The most great battle, the banquet of God, shall be witnessed on the plain of 'Akká." Also cited is his saying concerning the ministers of the Promised One: "They shall slay them all save one, who shall dwell upon the plain of 'Akká at the divine banquet, which God has made to be a table of feasting for beasts of prey, fowl, and vermin."[20] There are many more such sayings that God has concealed in the hidden reaches of His knowledge and reposited in the inner depths of the Qur'án's verses. The revolution of days and the passing of ages have amply confirmed them. His mention will extend to the ends of the earth, and His fame will fill the seven heavens.

Were those who reject everything beyond nature to be equitable, and were they to contemplate these abstruse matters, they would be forced to confess that human minds cannot perceive these matters in every detail and particular before their occurrence, nor can they inform the people of them before they come true. How can any knowledgeable and fair-minded person, given that this be the case, deny that from the Holy Reality, from the very Dawning-Places of the universal, all-encompassing Power, there might appear things that bewilder the reason, transcend the capacity of other souls, astonish the mind, and captivate the heart?

Therefore, it does not behoove us to speak at length in discussing the appearance from them of special miracles. Rather, we must explain the essence of miracles themselves and their division into two categories: signs proposed to the prophets and revealed written signs—as well as the degree to which each of these types constitutes a proof. Do proposed signs constitute proof of the truth of the prophets? To what extent are these a necessary attribute for their being, a sign of their theophany, a proof of the truth of their call, or a support for their word? Or does this quality of proof not inhere in them, such that it is not a necessary quality for them to show forth? We shall discuss this complex issue and overcome the burden of its difficulties.

Let us plunge into the deluge, and then we shall uncover its secrets. It is, by God, a stumbling block for the feet and a hotly contested issue among the world's people. Through their ignorance, many an ancient civilization fell, and oblivion was irrevocably decreed for many a past era.*

*In the essay beginning on p. 97 Mírzá Abú'l-Faḍl gives a full discussion of his views on miracles.

Part II

Commentary on "Then it is Ours to explain it."

(Qur'án 75:19)

MÍRZÁ ABU'L-FAḌL (left) WITH ALI-KULI KHAN

It will not have escaped those with clear vision that God has stated, in many places in the Qur'án, that there are interpretations of the verses which are known only to Him. This is indicated by the verse, "And none knows its interpretation, save only God," and, "Nay, they deny what their knowledge does not encompass, though its interpretation has not yet come to them."[1] The explanation for this is as follows: When the Glorious Book was revealed, it contained prophecies and predictions of events that would take place in the world, which all the nations were to see and witness. Similar prophecies are found in the Pentateuch, the Gospel, and the books of the minor prophets of the House of Israel. These include prophecies that the sun will be rolled up and cease to give its light, the moon darkened, the stars scattered, the heavens cleft asunder, and the earth and sky transformed. All parts of the heavens will be covered by smoke and split by clouds. They predict that the earth shall quake, the mountains turn to dust, the moon and the sun unite, and so forth.

These mighty verses are such that reason rejects them, and so it is difficult for many souls to admit the possibility that they might come to pass and to accept them. Indeed, the occurrence of such events is considered utterly impossible, as has been established by the natural sciences and in astronomy. The pagan, polytheistic Arabs used to deny all the prophets who appeared from the line of Abraham, such as Moses, Jesus, and Muḥammad. They, therefore, paid close attention to these verses and discussed them, engaging in disputes with the companions of the Prophet over their impossibility, in order to entice the believers away from Islam. They stated that Muḥammad was duping his people, deceiving his companions with verses such as these, promising them absurdities, raising false hopes, and convincing them of impossibilities. Then the above-mentioned verses were revealed. They indicate that the people only denied the verses of the noble Qur'án because the meaning was beyond their grasp and because they were ignorant of what was intended thereby. Actually, the meaning of those verses had not yet been revealed, and the interpretation of those statements had not yet been given to the people. This was precisely to alert them to the truth that these verses did possess rational significance, sublime meanings, and deliberately figurative interpretations. God would manifest these to them on a specified Day, after the expiration of a designated term. This is demonstrated by the verse, "Do they look for aught else but its interpretation? The day its interpretation comes, those who before forgot it shall say, 'Indeed, our Lord's messengers came with the truth. . . .'"[2]

It is obvious that the true interpretation of the verses of the Qur'án cannot be their literal meaning or their lexicological significance, which anyone who knows the Arabic language could comprehend. Otherwise, there would be no sense in the sacred verse: "And none knows its interpretation save God," or, "Nay, they deny what their knowledge does not encompass." Rather, the meaning of "interpretation" is the concealed significance with which He has endued these words through metaphors, similes, metonymies, and other figurative usages.

Were it not for the people's misunderstanding of these subtle meanings and sublime significances in past ages, the prophets would not have concealed them behind a veil of metaphors and would not have communicated them with esoteric allusions. Thus is it written in the thirteenth chapter of Matthew: "All this Jesus said to the crowds in parables; indeed he said nothing to them without a parable. This was to fulfill what was spoken by the prophet: 'I will open my mouth in parables, I will utter what has been hidden since the foundation of the world.'"[3] It is also recorded in the sixteenth chapter of the Gospel according to John that Jesus said to his disciples, "I have many things to say to you, but you cannot bear them now. When the spirit of truth comes, he will guide you into all the truth."[4] In the traditions of the Prophet are the sayings, "We, the concourse of prophets, were sent to address people according to the capacity of their minds," and in al-Bukhárí through 'Alí, "Speak to the people of that with which they are familiar; do you wish God and His Messenger to be called liars?"

It has been established that the world is advancing toward perfection, and that the spirits and hearts of men are certainly progressing toward the station of moderation and maturity. Thus they may one day attain to a level where they can understand the words of the prophets. This is required by the law of progress and advancement. God ordained that these verses be revealed from the tongues of the prophets, and He gave the task of unveiling their meaning and explaining their intent to the Spirit of God when he should descend from heaven. This was so that the hearts of the faithful might be strengthened and nurtured by the outward sense of the Holy Verses, so that the community might advance in the light of the true law, and so that the people might be enabled, in the meantime, to travel the far distances and to endure the extended interval between their own time and the expiration of the allotted term.

Shaykh Suhrawardí (may God sanctify his soul) said at the end of his book, *Temples of Light:*[5] "The insightful must believe in the soundness of the prophecies, and that their similarity is a proof of their reality. As it says in the Qur'án, 'And those similitudes—we strike them for the people, but none understands them save those who know,' and as some of the prophecies warn, 'I will open my mouth in a parable.'[6] Revelation was entrusted to the prophets, and its interpretation and elucidation were delegated to the most great, illumined, and bounteous Manifestation, the Comforter.[7] This is as Christ warned, saying, 'I am going to my Father and your Father, that He might send you the Comforter, who will inform you of the interpretation,' and, 'But the Comforter . . . whom the Father will send in my name, he shall teach you all things.'[8] This was alluded to in the Qur'án: 'Then it is Ours to explain it.'[9] and so forth. There is no doubt that the lights of the kingdom of heaven are descending to rescue the disconsolate. The radiance of holiness is spreading, and the path of truth is open, as the angry lightning informs us on a tempest-swept night." It is as God said, "It is He who looses the winds bearing good tidings with the hands of His mercy."[10]

From what has gone before, it is clear that all the prophets from Adam to their Seal, Muḥammad, came to reveal the above verses and to spread the traditional glad tidings without concerning themselves with explaining them. This was owing, as we have said, to the inability of the people to bear their meaning and their incapacity to perceive their purpose. These prophets were only sent to guide the masses to the desired goal. They were content if the people attained a general faith, until their Book reached the end of its dispensation and the advance of the hearts toward the level of maturity was completed. At that time the promised Spirit of God would appear and reveal the concealed realities to them on the Resurrection Day.

Those possessed of understanding know that the most difficult task for any accomplished scholar is to attempt to explain something to a person incapable of grasping it. For if a reality is revealed to one who cannot comprehend it, he will deny its truth because of his inability to understand. The tradition from al-Bukhárí we quoted above makes this clear: "Speak to the people of that with which they are familiar; do you wish God and His Messenger to be called liars?" The people would only end up in a state of unbelief after having had faith, and in apostasy after having obeyed. This contravenes the purpose for which the prophets were sent; it negates the plan prescribed for the chosen ones to follow. This is indicated by God's saying, "O believers, question not concerning things which, if they were revealed to you, would vex you."[11]

They asked the Prophet about those mysterious truths and abstruse meanings, but he found it difficult to explain these to them because, as we have already said, they were incapable of grasping these truths and unable to bear them. He thus forbade them to question him about them or to delve into them. Humanity's growth of comprehension, and its spiritual progress, is just like the course of bodily growth and physical progress. A human being must drink milk during his infancy, while his body is growing and before it attains perfection. During this time, eating coarse foods will certainly harm him, and, indeed, a cooked meal might kill him. In the same way, while his mind is growing and his comprehension is maturing, he needs at first simple, literal statements and would be destroyed by grappling with abstruse meanings.

From this, the difficulty the Prophet faced when the Qur'án was revealed can be understood, as can the stress he underwent when he recited the verses. For they used to question him concerning their true reality and significance, and he used to move his lips and try hard to find a way of elucidating to them. This was because of the difficulty of explaining something to a person incapable of grasping it, and the equal difficulty of abandoning the effort lest this be attributed to impotence. Then the verse was revealed, "Move not thy tongue with it to hasten it."[12] That is, to hasten the explanation of its hidden meanings and its mysterious interpretations. It continues, "Ours it is to gather it, and to recite it,"[13] (as God ordained that it later be gathered by the rightly guided caliphs, may God be pleased with them all).* He added, "Then Ours it is to explain it."[14] That is, when the community, because of its advancement by means of the holy Islamic law, attained the highest degree of perfection and when hearts became capable of grasping what is concealed in the Books of God, the All-Glorious, the Most High—then would the morn of attainment dawn, the Spirit descend in the clouds of glory, the mists of error be dispelled, and the Lord manifest Himself in the most glorious robes of beauty. He would explain to

*The official edition of the Qur'án was collected and published under the third caliph, 'U<u>th</u>mán (r. 644–656 A.D.). This was accomplished by a team of s<u>ch</u>olars under Zayd ibn <u>Th</u>ábit, probably between 650 and 656 A.D.

them the interpretation of the Book, reveal the quintessence of the divine Speech, and complete the bounty of God to His servants in every respect.

From what we have said, the meaning of the saying reported from Ibn 'Abbás is clear: "The Prophet—peace be upon him—used to undergo stress from receiving revelations, and would move his lips." Then he said, "I am moving mine as the Prophet used to move his."[15] For whenever any mature scholar is questioned by someone who is unable to grasp abstruse meanings, or is interrogated by someone who has never attained an understanding of sublime matters, he experiences stress and difficulty, stammers in his speech, faces the dilemma of attempting to make his questioner understand, and moves his lips in his utterance. It is not reasonable to maintain that this stress derived from the ringing of revelation, as some have interpreted this verse. For revelation involves no ringing, and ringing involves no difficulty. Revelation is only the descent of verses upon the breasts of prophets and messengers. This is shown by God's saying, "Nay; rather it is signs, clear signs in the breasts of those who have been given knowledge; and none denies Our signs but the evildoers," and "Brought down by the Faithful Spirit, upon thy heart, that thou mayest be one of the warners, in a clear Arabic tongue. Truly it is in the scriptures of the ancients."

Did the authors of those commentaries, which are hardly better than adolescent musings, think that the divine revelation, which the leaders of Sunní Islam term "the Preexistent Speech," consists of chains and bells, that it produces clanging and ringing? They depend for this view on some weak traditions and absurd ideas. How base their ruminations! How wretched is that to which they have compared the verses of God, despising and disdaining His words! How many calamities have these foolish commentaries brought upon the Holy Scriptures—opening the door to opposition, objection, refutation, and criticism of the divine words! See the "Discourse on Islam" written by the Englishman George Sale and the comments on it by Háshim ash-Shámí. Subject them to close scrutiny. The criticisms with which these two scholars attack the Qur'án derive in reality from the commentaries and glosses of interpreters. The absurdity of the latter can now become clear because of the swift progress that can be seen in the advancement of understanding and reason, and the expansion of the frontiers of knowledge and science. How many are the tribulations these criticisms and disputes have brought upon nations and religions! They have opened the gates of hatred and enmity. They have resulted in wars and attacks which have caused so much blood to be spilled that such treatises and essays as the present one cannot hope to describe it. Let us here close our discourse. Peace be upon the peacemakers, and upon those who open the doors of affection and love between all men.

Part III

The Alexandrian Epistle: Biblical Prophecies about Islam

ADORATION OF THE MAGI
Indian Painting, mid-seventeenth century. Courtesy of the Freer Gallery of Art, Smithsonian Institution, Washington, D.C.

He is the All-Powerful!

My beloved friend,* your letter reached me and gave me much joy. Your discourse delighted me, for I perceived in it the glittering lights of knowledge and mystical insight, and the lightning flashes of proof burst forth from the clouds of its strokes. I praised God, my Lord and yours, for having showered on you His spiritual bounties though you are in the vitality of your youth and in spite of the fewness of your years. He has generously conferred on you His compassionate blessings in the prime of your days and while your boughs are yet luxuriant. I beseech Him to extend your life, to confirm you in aiding the Cause of your Lord, and to inspire you to that which is best for you in this world and in the next.

You ask about passages in the Pentateuch and the Gospel that might be cited concerning the appearance of the Prophet Muḥammad. Know, my beloved friend,

*The eminent scholar Abú'l-Faḍl wrote this epistle in answer to a question from Ḥusayn Effendi Rúḥí. The latter asked him about places in the Holy Books where there are glad tidings of our lord the Prophet [Muḥammad], after he had been involved in a dispute with a priest over this matter.—Faraju'lláh Zakí al-Kurdí [who helped finance the publication of the first Arabic edition of this book]

[Ḥusayn Rúḥí (1878–1960) was the son of Ḥájj 'Alí Tabrízí, a Bahá'í teacher sent to Egypt by Bahá'u'lláh. For his biography, see *The Bahá'í World: An International Record*, vol. 13 (Haifa: The Universal House of Justice, 1970), pp. 938–39.]

that anyone who carefully examines all the Holy Scriptures will see that all such books contain two kinds of teachings. The first category contains the laws and ordinances the community will need over the period of its existence, and on which its success and propserity will depend. The second category is the prophecies concerning the advent of the Day of God, the descent of the Spirit of God [Jesus], and the appearance of the Manifestation of the Cause of God. This Day is the great, terrible, and awful Day that has been referred to in the heavenly scriptures by various expressions, by such exalted names as the Day of the Lord, the Day of the Kingdom, the Day of Affliction, the Day of the Meeting, the Resurrection, the Hour, and so forth. The prophets stipulated conditions for the advent of that Day and mentioned signs, tokens, indications, proofs, and prerequisites for it. These are recorded in the ancient books and are clearly stated in these scriptures.

Know, my beloved friend, that it can be inferred from some books that since an ancient time whose beginnings remain unknown, the prophets have given the people the glad tidings that the Cause of God will come, and the dawn of the Day of God will break. Then will the gloom of disputes, heresies, wars, and hatreds between His servants be dispelled. However, owing to the obscurity of ancient histories, the lack of information about peoples in times past, the difficulty of preserving scholarly works (because printed works, paper, and so forth, were easily lost in those days), and the lack of cooperation, mutual aid, and acquaintance between ancient tribes, insufficient information can be had about the prophecies made by the prophets before Moses. For no book by them has survived and no traditions exist, that an inquirer might benefit from their contents or inform himself of the stipulations of their prophecies. This being the case, we have no choice but to consider the Pentateuch the first Holy Book whose passages may be drawn upon, and from whose reflections the intended meaning may be gleaned.

Let us first of all begin with the verses of the Pentateuch, then proceed to the sayings contained in the books of the prophets of Israel, and conclude with the glad tidings found in the Gospel. We place our trust in God: He, verily is the best of Lords and the best of Guardians.

God said, according to Deuteronomy 33:2: "The Lord came from Sinai, and dawned from Seir upon us; he shone from Mount Paran, he came from the ten thousands of holy ones, with flaming fire at his right hand." This blessed verse clearly indicates that before the striking of the Hour, and before the advent of the Resurrection, God will reveal Himself to His creation four times and will unveil four Manifestations. Only then will the generations of the children of Israel be completed, will they attain to the glorious Lord, will their scattered remnants be gathered together from the remotest lands, will they be protected from harm by mankind. Only then will they be settled in the Holy Land and will their ancient legacy be returned to them.

In accordance with this noble verse, there first appeared Moses. God became manifest to them by His Theophany from Mt. Sinai. Second, Jesus appeared, and God revealed Himself from Mt. Seir. Third, Muḥammad arose, and God was effulgent from Mt. Paran. Then ages passed, and nights and days followed one another until the Chosen Lord manifested Himself and the fourth theophany was completed by the decree of the King, the All-Glorious, the All-Compelling.

There is no substance to the arguments of some

who refute this verse's relevance by saying that the words "dawned," "shone forth," and "came" occur in the past tense, and that if this verse were a prediction of four theophanies these would have been in the future tense. For the prophecies of the Holy Books, even of the noble Qur'án, often occur in the past tense as an evidence that their content must inevitably come to pass and is decisively true. There is for instance the verse, ". . . and thy Lord came, and the angels rank on rank."[1] See also the fourteenth verse of the Letter of St. Jude, where the past is used to mean the future: "It was of these also that Enoch in the seventh generation from Adam prophesied, saying, 'Behold, the Lord came with his holy myriads.'"[2] But in fact, the interval between Enoch (who, historians have established, is the Prophet Idris) and Jesus is greater than the distance separating Moses from Muḥammad.[3]

See also Deuteronomy 18:18, where God says, "I will raise up for them a prophet like you from among their brethren; and I will put my words in his mouth, and he shall speak to them all that I command him." That this refers to the appearance of Muḥammad is more likely than that it refers to Jesus, as some have attempted to maintain. For the Quraysh tribe is from the progeny of Ishmael. They are the "brethren" of the Hebrews in terms of lineage, since the Jews are descendants of Israel. Ishmael and Isaac were the two sons of Abraham: the Arabs appeared from the progeny of Ishmael, while the children of Israel came from the line of Isaac. The Arabs are therefore the brethren of the children of Israel, in genealogical terms.

As for Jesus' descent from Abraham, we have as yet found no dependable evidence for this. The Jews themselves, who were the people of his House, denied Jesus' relation to them and claimed that he was a Samaritan. This is shown by John 8:48: "The Jews answered him, 'Are we not right in saying you are a Samaritan and have a demon?'" This passage provides clear evidence that the children of Israel at that time, when their genealogies were still preserved and recognized, did not consider him one of them. They did not accept him as having the same origin as they. They were the people of the house, and as the proverb has it, "The people of the house know best what is therein."

No consideration can be given to the genealogies in the Gospels according to Matthew and Luke relating him to David, since the chains of descent in these two genealogies contain disparities.[4] Matthew related Jesus to David through Solomon; and Luke through Nathan, Solomon's brother, which is altogether unreasonable. This is not to speak of the disparities in the number and names of the individuals mentioned in these two genealogies. Many attempts have been made to correct this error with unlikely interpretations. However, these are more likely to provoke laughter than to silence the skeptic, and more likely to raise doubts for a critic than to convince him. An earnest, critical inquirer will pay no attention to such attempts, except to doubt them and dismiss them.

Moreover, Christians do not consider Jesus a prophet. Rather, they hold him to be the only Son of God—and more, the third person of the Trinity which they believe constitutes God's essence. Therefore, this prophecy clearly does not apply to him.

In 1305 A.H. [1887–88 A.D.], when I was in Hamadan, I heard a Jewish rabbi of the line of Levi, who had taken refuge with the Mighty Pillar and cleaved to the Glorious Cord of God. He said, "This prophecy applies solely to the appearance of Muḥammad, for there is perfect resemblance between the Islamic and Jewish religions with respect to their legislation, lineage, laws, origins, beginnings, ordainers, and founders. They are thus twin branches of one tree, two sprouts from the same root."

He then recited Isaiah 63:1: "Who is this that comes from Edom, in crimsoned garments from Bozrah, he that is glorious in his apparel, marching in the greatness of his strength?" When he had recited the entire chapter, he said, "These verses warned with the greatest frankness of the calamities that befell the children of Israel at the appearance of Islam. For God forewarned them that a divine and heavenly man would come from Edom, which is the land falling between Palestine and Arabia; and Bozrah is one of its cities. It is also called Buṣrá of Silks. The Arabian Prophet, with his uncle, Abú Ṭálib, came to the coasts of Syria twice before his manifestation. It was in Syria that Baḥírá' the monk said to Abú Ṭálib, 'A great future lies before this nephew of yours . . . guard him carefully against his enemies.'[5] The caliphs of Islam conquered Syria and dispersed the children of Israel. The prophecies of this chapter must refer solely to the Prophet Muḥammad, for Jesus did not come from Edom and never entered the city of Bozrah; so these predictions do not apply to him."

In the eighth verse of this chapter, it is written: "For he said, 'Surely they are my people, sons who will not deal falsely; and he became their Savior. In all their affliction he was afflicted, and the angel of his presence saved him; in his love and in his pity he redeemed them; he lifted them up and carried them all the days of old. But they rebelled and grieved his holy

Spirit; therefore he turned to be their enemy, and himself fought against them."[6] Truly, anyone who reads this passage will see clearly that it contains prophecies concerning the three cycles which the children of Israel underwent during three dispensations. For he said that his people were the children of Israel, and he lifted them up and carried them all the days of old—that is, in the dispensation of Moses. But they grieved his holy Spirit, that is, in the dispensation of Jesus. For Jesus is the true Spirit of God, and the Jews grieved him and denied him. They dared to insult him and to curse him, and they decreed his death. Then the Spirit of God turned to be their enemy and fought against them, that is, in the dispensation of Muḥammad. For he fought against them in the raid on the Qurayẓah clan, when nine hundred of their men were killed in a single day. His caliphs expelled them from Syria, abolished their sacrifices, and forbade them to perform their rituals, as one can see in the histories. Because of fatigue and lack of space, this must suffice as a mention of the prophecies about Muḥammad's appearance in the Old Testament. We beseech God to aid us in completing this proof on another occasion. He is, verily, our Protector in the beginning and in the end.

Now for glad tidings of the Prophet's advent in the New Testament. Know, my beloved friend, that a human being cannot reach the station of prophet, messenger, or legislator, nor attain unto divinity, unless a holy and celestial potency manifests itself in the temple of his body and a sanctified and divine spirit descends upon the throne of his heart. When this holy power becomes refulgent in the heart of a human being, when this heavenly bestowal descends upon his breast, when this divine breeze wafts over his soul, and this celestial potency rests on him, then he is called the Prophet of God, the Messenger of God, the Word of God, the Most Exalted Countenance, the Loftiest Heaven, the Tree beyond which there is no passing, and the Ultimate Goal. "Whichsoever you call upon, to Him belong the Most Beautiful Names."[7]

However, this station is bestowed, not acquired; it is given as a confirmation, not learned; and it is heavenly, not earthly. It is a single reality which is not multiplied by numerous manifestations, a single light that does not divide, even though it often shines forth, and a single effulgence that does not vary with the difference of the Easts and Wests. Should it be manifest upon Sinai, it is that same divine potency; if it shines from Seir, it is that same heavenly pearl; and if it dawns from Paran, it is that same godly star. If it wafts from Persia, it is that same spiritual breeze; and if it glows, flares, shimmers, and scintillates from Ṭihrán, it is that same, single Sun of Reality. It has always been effulgent from all eternity, and its lights shall forever continue to gleam forth throughout the coming generations and centuries.

By your life, my friend! The affirmation of God's unity has no meaning save the recognition of this subtle point, and no man can escape the evil darkness of those who have joined partners with God save by attaining this noble goal. Moses alluded to this truth when he said, "For I lift up my hand to heaven and swear, As I live forever."[8] Jesus referred to it, saying, "I am the Alpha and the Omega . . . the beginning and the end."[9] Muḥammad also pointed to it in the tradition, "The first thing God created was my light." 'Alí said in this regard, "Verily, we are the first ones, the harbingers of this world and the next, the signs of all times. Whoever perished, perished by us; whoever was saved, was saved by us."

Know that the prophecies Jesus made concerning his return and Second Coming, which are recorded in many Gospel verses, were first of all fulfilled by the appearance of Muḥammad, by virtue of that essential unity we have mentioned above. The appearance of this Messenger of God truly represented the return of the Spirit of God, Jesus. In the same way, all the works, deeds, power, and potency that Jesus manifested were also shown forth by Muḥammad. No importance can be attached to the multiplicity of Manifestations and bodies, for bodies are but instruments whereby spirits display their works. The pivotal factor in the realization of the divine essence is the spirit, not the body.

An example of this appears in the Gospel, where Jesus pronounced John the Baptist to be Elijah the Prophet.[10] However, both Jews and Christians agree that Elijah ascended to heaven nearly nine hundred years before John the Baptist.[11] If Jesus could declare that John the Baptist was Elijah—in spite of the difference in their names, times, lineages, forms, and bodies—because of their unity in spirit, then why cannot a scholarly researcher conclude that by the descent of the Son of Man was intended the appearance of Muḥammad? For exactly the same spiritual unity and essential harmony existed between them. Moreover, John the Baptist himself denied that he was Elijah, as is clearly stated in John 1:19–23. However, Muḥammad never denied that he was the reality of the past prophets and messengers. Indeed, the verses "Our command is but one, like the twinkling of an eye" and "We make no division between any one of His Messengers" openly demonstrate that he is the reality of all the prophets and messengers, and his appearance represents the return of all those who came before. "Surely in that are signs for such as mark."[12]

By your life, my friend! I do not marvel that the people of the East were given pause by such ambiquities, found themselves impotent to grasp these points, and remained ignorant of the true meaning of these verses. This is because of their deficient understanding of natural science and astronomy. However, I am astonished, bewildered, and dumbfounded by those who believe themselves to be natural philosophers, astronomers, well-versed doctors, and mature scholars. They have measured the heavens cubit by cubit and weighed it particle by particle. They have discovered the constituent parts of the earthly elements and fathomed their natural mysteries. How then can they accept things that are rationally untenable and completely impossible? How can they wait expectantly for things that contradict the ways of God from ancient times?

Where are there composed minds, understanding hearts, sharp eyes, even dispositions, apposite perceptions, and serene understandings? Have all natures grown foolish? Have all feet stumbled? Have they forgotten God's ways in past times and days? Have the souls, after the world has ascended so high on the ladder of progress, degenerated into the skepticism of extinct peoples or sunk into the abyss of the idle fancies of the ancients? Do they expect anything but the path of those who passed away before them? "Say: Then watch and wait, verily I shall be with you watching and waiting."[13]

To realize that by the descent of the Son of Man was intended the return of that Holy Reality who is essentially one in all respects, is to recognize that this occurred when Muḥammad appeared. However, God had certain foreknowledge that the people of this age, in spite of their ample claims to progress and advancement, would fall into the same pit of doubt as had the ancients, and would cling to the same cord of vain imaginations as had their predecessors. He therefore desired to invalidate their proofs and useless fancies lest the people have any proof against God.

He therefore revealed in the Revelation of St. John prophecies of the Prophet Muḥammad's appearance and openly proclaimed in this noble Book all the events associated with his dispensation, and that which would befall his community till the Resurrection Day.

It is recorded in the eleventh chapter of that book:

> And I will grant my two witnesses power to prophesy for one thousand two hundred and sixty days, clothed in sackcloth. These are the two olive trees and the two lampstands which stand before the Lord of the earth. And if anyone would harm them, fire pours from their mouth and consumes their foes; if any one would harm them, thus is he doomed to be killed. They have power to shut the sky, that no rain may fall during the days of their prophesying, and they have power over the waters to turn them into blood, and to smite the earth with every plague, as often as they desire. And when they have finished with their testimony, the beast that ascends from the bottomless pit will make war upon them and conquer them and kill them, and their dead bodies will lie in the street of the great city which is allegorically called Sodom and Egypt, where their Lord was crucified. For three days and a half men from the peoples and tribes and tongues and nations gaze at their dead

bodies and refuse to let them be placed in a tomb, and those who dwell on the earth will rejoice over them and make merry and exchange presents, because these two prophets had been a torment to those who dwell on the earth. But after the three and a half days a breath of life from God entered them, and they stood up on their feet, and great fear fell on those who saw them. Then they heard a loud voice from heaven saying to them, "Come up hither!" And in the sight of their foes they went up to heaven in a cloud. And at that hour there was a great earthquake, and a tenth of that city fell; seven thousand people were killed in the earthquake, and the rest were terrified and gave glory to the God of heaven.

The second woe has passed; behold, the third woe is soon to come.

Then the seventh angel blew his trumpet, and there were loud voices in heaven, saying, "The kingdom of the world has become the kingdom of our Lord and of his Christ, and he shall reign for ever and ever. And the twenty-four elders who sit on their thrones before God fell on their faces and worshiped God, saying, 'We give thanks to thee, Lord God Almighty, who art and wast, that thou hast taken thy great power and begun to reign. The nations raged, but thy wrath came, and the time for the dead to be judged, for rewarding thy servants, the prophets and saints, and those who fear thy name, both small and great, and for destroying the destroyers of the earth.'" Then God's temple in heaven was opened, and the ark of his covenant was seen within his temple; and there were flashes of lightning, loud noises, peals of thunder, an earthquake, and heavy hail.[14]

As you see, the words of this chapter state and proclaim that after St. John, to whom these prophecies were revealed, God would raise up two heavenly witnesses, that is, two divine men, who would call the people to the religion of God. They would bear witness and confess to the truth of Jesus' resurrection. You know that after the ascent of Jesus into the heavens of God's presence (or, to put it more clearly, from the time these revealed prophecies descended) until the dawn of the morn of the Day of God, no one arose with prophethood or guardianship to bear witness to the unity of God and to the truth of His prophets and messengers, from Adam to Christ, save our Lord Muḥammad. And the gate to the city of his knowledge was 'Alí. These two resplendent luminaries, these blessed olive trees, arose to proclaim the unity of God and the truth of His Messiah. Through their witness, great nations became believers, though they had not formerly recognized the oneness of God or the truth of Christ Jesus, the Spirit of God, but rather worshiped fire and idols. They came to believe and obey; they assented and attained certitude.

In this way the divine revelation was fulfilled, and the vision of John the Divine became a reality. After they completed their witness, their light spread and their word was established. Then appeared the frightful beast, that is, the vicious monarchy, the despotic caliphate of the Umayyads. The leadership of this Quray<u>sh</u>í clan, the kings of the Umayyad caliphate, fought against them. Abú Sufyán made war on the Prophet; Mu'áwiyah contended with 'Alí and poisoned Ḥasan; Yazíd waged war with Ḥusayn; Hi<u>sh</u>ám ibn 'Abdu'l-'Azíz struck at Zaynu'l-'Ábidín, the son of Ḥusayn. Thus, every single member of this pure, prophetic clan and this blessed, 'Alid family was poisoned or killed by the order of one of these tyrannical Umayyad caliphs.*

It is firmly established and plainly stated in the pages of the history books that when Ḥusayn, the son of 'Alí, was killed by the order of Yazíd, they imprisoned the people of his household and carried them, barefaced and bareheaded, on packsaddles to Damascus. Among them were daughters of the Messenger of God, and Fáṭimah's own children. They delivered them in this state into the city of Damascus. The people of that metropolis (metaphorically called Sodom) issued into the streets to look upon the Prophet's daughters, bareheaded and weeping and swung over the humps of camels. The heads of martyrs were carried aloft before them on spears and lances.

The people of Damascus celebrated as a festival the day the family of the Prophet arrived in chains. They cheered and laughed, and cursed and swore, owing to the bitterness they had nursed in their breasts from the battles of Badr, Uḥud, Ḥunayn, and Ṣiffín.† They refused to allow the heads of these martyrs to be buried, but circulated them throughout Syria so the people might rejoice at this clear victory. This they did for the three and a half years of the days of Yazíd's caliphate.‡

*This is a reference to the holy imams, relatives of the Prophet Muḥammad, who are accepted by Shí'í Muslims as his true successors.

†Badr (624 A.D.) and Uḥud (625 A.D.) were battles fought by the Muslims against their opponents, the Meccan polytheists. Ḥunayn (630 A.D.) was a large battle fought by the Muslims against a confederation of polytheist tribes after the Muslim conquest of Mecca. Ṣiffín (657 A.D.) was a battle between the Imám 'Alí's supporters and those of the usurper Mu'áwiyah.

‡He has interpreted three and a half days as three and a half years following the scriptural convention that a day with the Lord is a year.—FARAJU'LLÁH ZAKÍ AL-KURDÍ

[See Num. 14:34].

Finally, these remains were laid to rest in a Syrian city, where they remained until the Fáṭimid caliphate.* The Fáṭimid rulers then brought them to Egypt and ordered them interred here, where the people visit them even to this day. All the decline, the abasement, the degradation that has accrued to the Islamic community, and its conquest by its enemies, as you see today, is a direct result of this despotic caliphate, these tyrants of the past. This is indicated by God's saying, "We made the vision that We showed thee and the tree cursed in the Qur'án to be only a trial for men; and We frighten them, but it only increases them in great insolence."[15]

By your life, my beloved friend! A tree watered by pure blood will produce only the thorns of decline and loss; it will bear no fruit save the bitter-apples of ignominy and humiliation. The great scholar al-Fírúzábádí, the author of *al-Qámús* [Dictionary], said concerning the word *wadq* (and these two verses are the only ones extant by 'Alí ibn Abí Ṭálib):

> That is the Quraysh; they want me, to kill me.
> But no, by thy Lord, they did not obey and did not conquer.
> Should I be destroyed, then my honor is their ransom.
> By the double calamity [*wadqayn*], no trace of it shall be obliterated.[16]

Therefore, he said, a *wadq* is a calamity. As you can see, this double calamity has taken the form of external and internal afflictions: heedlessness, estrange-

*The Fáṭimids were a Shí'í dynasty of the Ismá'ílí sect, which reigned in North Africa, and later in Egypt, from 909 to 1171 A.D. As Shí'ís, or partisans of 'Alí, they naturally had much affection for Ḥusayn, 'Alí's martyred son.

ment, and apathy within, and the cunning, plotting, and fanaticism of enemies from without.

When Yazíd died, 'Alí Zaynu'l-'Ábidín, the son of Ḥusayn, returned to Medina. His presence restored the imamate, and the doors of guidance were flung open a second time upon his companions. The Umayyad and 'Abbásid caliphs always feared the Prophet's family, and they watched and spied on them. They harrassed them one by one until 260 A.H. [874 A.D.], when the imamate ended. Then the paths of guidance were concealed, the pure souls ascended to the highest heavens, and the darkest gloom of night reigned over all. Centuries and cycles followed one another. Finally, the secrets of the scriptures were unveiled, and the call of the sunrise was heard in all regions. Now that the sun is gone from view and the Book of the Covenant has been recited to the righteous, one can see that the clouds of doubt are gathering, the thunder of covenant-breaking and faithlessness is crashing, and the hail of skepticism and uncertainty is raining down.[17] In this way, the glad tidings have been fulfilled, the prophecies have come to pass, and the clear signs have appeared. The Cause is God's, the Sovereign of earth and heaven.

I would like to relate to you a humorous anecdote about the dispute that I had with a priest concerning the interpretation of this chapter of the Gospel—though I admit that this contravenes the principle of conciseness on which this essay has so far been based. I stopped over, in 1312 A.H. [1894–95 A.D.], in Syria and laid down my walking cane in the presence of the Lord of the Righteous* and the Point of Adoration for the free. May God enable me to hold firm to the cord

*A reference to 'Abdu'l-Bahá.

of fidelity to him as long as there be day and night! There one day I met Abú Nimrúd, an erudite minister of the Evangelical community, in the house of my beloved friend, Dr. Raphael.

We became engrossed in a discussion of how to vindicate the authenticity of the Prophet Muḥammad's mission. He asked me to establish a proof for this. I answered that the rational evidence, the decisive, conclusive proof, and the signal miracle which will verify the truthfulness of any man's divine claim is the transcendent potency he demonstrates in promulgating his Word, establishing his religion, and perpetuating his law in spite of the opposition of all the nations, and in the face of the combined forces of all the world's peoples. This is a potency no other force can surpass, with which no power can compete, and which no might or solidarity can ever conquer. For it does not derive from the limited and recognized sources of human power such as outward, earthly sovereignity or authority, acquired knowledge or science, financial wealth or fortune, communal ties or solidarity, or from worldly glory or leadership.

This power rests upon an invisible, divine potency and emanates from a heavenly, celestial force. This force, in turn, ultimately derives from the Necessarily Existent, the Cause of causes,* which all investigators must recognize, even the philosophers—those who believe in causes and factors. Without this, the skeptic and denier will be compelled to wander astray in the darkness of vain imaginations, and to reject self-evident, primary propositions. He will cleave to logical fallacies such as circular reasoning, infinite chains of causation, the affirmation of the cause, and

*That is, God.

so forth. This is a clear proof for all prophets and messengers; it is an obvious criterion which distinguishes between truthful and mendacious claimants. All this is to say that the more recently a messenger has appeared, the more manifest and powerful his proof will be. This is in accordance with the law of progress and advancement.

The minister responded that rational evidence is not considered dependable proof by Christians. He requested that I present evidence from the verses of the Old Testament and from the Gospel, as these are the bases among them for the establishment of proofs and evidence.

I replied, "If you do not consider rational evidence something to be concerned with, then you will be incapable of vindicating the truth of our lord Jesus to those who do not accept the validity of the Old Testament, such as the Buddhists, Hindus, and Zoroastrians. They do not know of Moses, and they do not recognize that the Old Testament is the Book of God, whose verses can be cited as evidence, and whose glad tidings can be presented as proof. How then will you establish and prove the truth of Christ to them? This is a sure sign that you are ignorant of the very meaning of proof and is an indication of your incapacity to attain a knowledge of the true path. Nevertheless, I will make this concession to you and quote for you some of the prophecies of the New Testament."

I recited for him the above-mentioned chapter and said to him, "These noble verses prophesy the arising of two great witnesses to God and to the truth of Christ. Muḥammad and his eminent son-in-law and disciple arose to proclaim and attest the unity of God and the truth of our lord Jesus."

He responded, saying, "This is not the meaning of

witnessing. Muḥammad should have borne witness that Jesus rose from the dead, saved the world, and redeemed all nations."

I said to him, "How is it that he has saved and redeemed all the peoples of the world, when you believe that most of the nations have persisted in a state of perdition until this very day? Let me ask you about them, nation by nation, lest we cleave to an illusion or rejoice for nothing. God be our witness, Abú Nimrúd, did our lord Jesus save the great Buddhist nation?"

He replied, "No."

I continued, "Then did he save the Hindu nation?"

He said, "No."

I asked, "Did he save the Zoroastrian nation or the pagan nations,[18] or even the Jewish nation?"

He responded, "No."

"Then," I suggested, "let us speak of the Christian peoples. As God is our witness, did he save the Catholics?"

He said, "No."

"Did he," I wondered, "save the Easten Orthodox peoples?"

"No."

"Did he save the Jacobites, the Nestorians, the Melkites, or the others who are not Protestants?"

"No."

I concluded, "Then only the Evangelicals are left. And, no doubt, you believe that only the righteous among them are saved and redeemed. Yet this is a tiny portion of the world's peoples. How, then, can your assertion that he rose from the dead and saved all the peoples of the world be true? And were anyone to bear this witness, how could any rational person accept it?

"As for us," I continued, "our forefathers, the mighty nations of Persia, Arabia, Turkey, Gílán, and others too numerous to mention, used to worship fire and adore idols. They did not recognize the unity of God and did not know of Moses or Jesus. However, by the witness of this chosen messenger and appointed prophet they came to believe that there is no God but God, that Moses conversed with God, and that Jesus is the Spirit of God. We inherited this pure creed from generation to generation, preserved it in our breasts, and inscribed love for these messengers upon our hearts. No one can deny this. This is a veracious witness and a clear prophethood."

He replied, "Yes, surely. But these peoples will never attain the bounty of salvation, owing to their lack of faith. Should they believe, they would be redeemed. Salvation depends upon faith."

I answered, "Then, salvation has not occurred and redemption has failed. This being so, it is not true to bear witness that Jesus rose and saved the world. And so, first of all, how can you demand that the Prophet Muḥammad bear this witness? Second, the dependence of salvation upon faith is not confined to the case of Christ. Rather, this is true in the case of every messenger and has been true of all the prophets. Had all the people believed in Moses, would he not have redeemed them all from perdition? Has not each prophet been sent to guide the people? Is not the meaning of guidance to show them the path of salvation and to guide them to the road of redemption? This is not something confined or specially granted to our lord Jesus. God would not, therefore, raise up two great witnesses to attest to something that, in the first place, never happened, and in the second, was not confined to him." At that point, our discussion ended and we went our separate ways in peace.

Let us now return from this lengthy digression to our quotation of the New Testament's prophecies. It is recorded in the twelfth chapter of the Book of Revelation:

> And a great portent appeared in heaven, a woman clothed with the sun, with the moon under her feet, and on her head a crown of twelve stars; she was with child and she cried out in her pangs of birth, in anguish for delivery. And another portent appeared in heaven; behold a great red dragon, with seven heads and ten horns, and seven diadems upon his heads. His tail swept down a third of the stars of heaven, and cast them to the earth. And the dragon stood before the woman who was about to bear a child, that he might devour her child when she brought it forth; she brought forth a male child, one who is to rule all the nations with a rod of iron, but her child was caught up to God and to his throne, and the woman fled into the wilderness, where she has a place prepared by God, in which to be nourished for one thousand two hundred and sixty days.

Know, my beloved friend, that whenever an animal or beast is mentioned in prophecies, this refers to kings and states. Moreover, as can be gathered from the holy Book of Certitude, the Kitáb-i-Íqán, often "heavens" refers to the heavens of God's Cause and the heavens of religion.[19] "Sun" symbolizes the Sun of Reality, that is, the Holy Power, the Divine Spirit, and the Prophetic Reality. "Moon" means the noble Branch that came forth from the Ancient Root, that is, the first satellite that rises in the heaven of the Cause after the Sun has set, which is called the moon of succession or the luminary of the imamate. "Stars" refers to the stars of the heaven of religion, and the heavenly lights in the sphere of certitude, including the temperate, the righteous, the martyrs, and the upright.

Moreover, the meaning of the woman clothed with the sun in this prophecy is Fáṭimah, the daughter of the Prophet. She is the glorious, noble, prophetic pearl whom the Messenger of God married to the moon of succession and the daystar of the heaven of guidance, the Commander of the Faithful, 'Alí ibn Abí Ṭálib. He covenanted and declared that the Mahdí of the Prophet's House, who, as the will of God had foreordained, would fill the world with equity and justice after it had been filled with tyranny and despotism, would appear from the lineage of these two radiant lights, this noble couple. God adorned the splendid crown of Fáṭimah with twelve stars, who were cynosures of guidance and moons of succession. These were the twelve imams, whose virtues have covered pages and filled tomes, and whose goodly traits became renowned to all the horizons, in spite of what the hand of tyranny and discord covered up, and what the artifices of despotism and hypocrisy concealed.

By the great dragon with seven heads and ten horns is meant the lawless Umayyad caliphate and the vicious Marwánid monarchy. The horns are the kings of that dynasty, and the heads are their senior appointees, the vastness of whose conquests the pens of flatterers yet celebrate, and the multitude of whose slaves, including captives and prisoners from various lands, the tongues of braggarts still vaunt. They do not realize that all the bitter torment the Muslim community is tasting in our own time is a consequence of this torrential flood of dictatorship, this frightful tempest of destruction. Whoever compares the speech made by Ṭáriq ibn Ziyád when he conquered Spain, with the ode written by Sayyid Yaḥyá of Córdoba when this realm passed out of the hands of the Muslims, will see that there was a poetic justice in this retribution.* War gives rise only to war, even if this requires centuries and generations.

By the tail of the dragon is intended the generals of these despotic caliphs and tyrannical kings, for they used to persecute the descendants of the Prophet. They killed every righteous man among the Muslims. Al-Ḥajjáj, the notorious oppressor should suffice you in this regard. He alone would allow the Umayyads to surpass all other kings of the world, should these ever boast of having had martinets for governors and butchers for generals.[20] The flame of his sword scorched mankind; the fire of his transgression spared no one. I read in a well-regarded chronicle (I think is was *Gold-washings and Mines of Gems*)[21] that K͟hálid ibn Yazíd, Mu'áwiyah's grandson, was passing through a side-street in Damascus and met al-Ḥajjáj in the road. When K͟hálid saw him, he lauded him as another 'Amr ibn al-'Áṣ, with poetry celebrating his slyness and cunning.† Ḥajjáj haughtily rejected this comparison of himself with 'Amr. He replied to K͟hálid, "I have slain with my sword a hundred thousand Muslims who used to bear witness to your father's unbelief." That is, he used to serve the Umayyads, and in order to build up their kingdom, slew ten times as many Muslims as 'Amr ever did. How then could K͟hálid demean him by such a comparison? Among those murdered by the order of Ḥajjáj was Sa'íd ibn Jubayr.

*Muslims ruled Spain from about 722 A.D. until they were finally expelled by Christian armies in 1492.

†'Amr ibn al-'Áṣ (d. 663 A.D.) was a contemporary of Muḥammad from the powerful Quraysh clan who at first opposed Islam and then converted in 629–30 A.D. He played an important part in the Arab conquest of Palestine and Egypt. Later, he supported the Umayyad usurper Mu'áwiyah against the Imám 'Alí, who was then caliph, and led troops against him at Ṣiffín.

He was a renowned holy man who had few peers among the Muslims. From what we have said, you can understand the meaning of the words "His tail swept down a third of the stars of heaven, and cast them to the earth."[22]

The child she brought forth, who was to rule all the nations with a rod of iron, was Ḥusayn. He was caught up to God and His throne through martyrdom. Whoever refers to the discourses of the Commander of the Faithful, and the oral traditions from the House of the Prophet, will recognize the intent of our lord Jesus' prophecy. This prophecy contains intricate allusions, exalted subtleties, and sublime meanings. We shall, however, refrain from elucidating them at this point, owing to lack of space and opportunity, and shall postpone this task to another occasion, God willing.

Since you are in the prime of your youth and at the beginning of your education, you should know that debate and investigation have rules and laws that must be observed. Otherwise, you may push the questioner away from the truth, the matter may result in the opposite of what you intended, and concealed feuds and hatreds may break out afresh. The wise debater must show respect to his opponent and must give consideration to his feelings. He must not harm him with harsh references or injure his feelings with cutting statements. The goal for both parties should be to gain enlightenment one from another, not to revile or defeat the other in argument. Should the scholar hear from his opponent a spiteful phrase or a brutal remark, he must receive it with forgiveness and forbearance and must treat him courteously, with love and faithfulness, so as to bring him nearer to the truth and remove the veil of ignorance from his heart. Otherwise, the affair will certainly end in wrangling and quarreling, rancor will be enkindled in the breasts of men, and in the end they will find themselves at war and in a vicious struggle.

It is well known that the gates of horrible warfare between nations have been flung open after religious disputes have broken out between them. The feelings of the two sides are injured by abusive tongues in scholarly quarrels. The leaders of the religious communities fix quills upon their pens to record their rebuttals, objections, exposés, and opposition to those whom the religions and denominations venerate. They write down all the lies and slander they can find about the founders of holy Causes and the ordainers of religions. Finally, the breasts grow agitated and the souls boil over. The war of words is transformed into a war of swords. The lines of pages become ranks of soldiers. Innocent blood is spilled, and civilized countries are reduced to rubble. No one can have any idea of the hideousness of such a scene, or the horror of its meaning, unless he has traveled throughout the regions, visited great cities, wandered through distant climes, and seen with his own eyes the aftermath of war, which most only read about in books. He stands upon forlorn ruins and amidst desolate rubble and weeps for what has come to pass because of impudent tongues and reckless pens.

I will never forget the bewilderment and confusion that gripped me when, in 1892 A.D., I visited the city of Shahristán in Turkmenistan, with some Russian officers. We gazed upon that city, which once produced the great scholar Muḥammad ash-Shahrastání, the author of the book *Religious Communities and Creeds.*[23] It was devastated, desolate, leveled, and barren, inhabited only by foxes and rats. No one passed by it but Turkoman pastoral nomads. Truly, anyone who travels to Khwarazm and sees the desert (which it takes a Russian train about two days and nights to traverse, from the Caspian Sea to the Syr River, then passing through Bukhara and Samarkand) will witness nothing except the remains of former metropolises and the ruins of famous cities. These include Jurján, Nasmá', Darún, Abívard, Shahristán, Merv, and other capitals that once flourished with knowledge and science, and prospered with trades and crafts. Indeed, they were the refuge of civilization and culture, the birthplace of branches of the caliphate and the emirates.

These cities became desolate and ruined after the horrible and bloody battles that took place in them because of sectarian disputes between Sunní and Shí'í Muslims. Their street ran with blood, nearby villages were razed, and so many infants were orphaned, so many women and girls taken prisoner, that those who count could never reckon them. Now all that can be seen is empty, fallow countryside; deserted, barren farmland; worn and eerie ruins. Surely God, in His eternal justice and with His irrevocable decree, will visit retribution upon those divines who opened the gates of enmity between peoples, filled their hearts with hostility and hatred, and aroused aversion and antipathy in their breasts. It is they who were responsible for the blood that was spilled, the honor that was ravished, the countries that were destroyed, and the villages and farms that were rendered barren.

For a reasonable man, some verses of the Qur'án will suffice to epitomize all we have been saying: "But the parties have fallen into variance among themselves; then woe to those who disbelieve for the scene of a dreadful day. How well they will hear and see on the day they come to Us! But the evildoers even today are in error manifest. Warn thou them of the day of anguish, when the matter shall be determined, and they yet heedless and unbelieving."[24]

I have always sought an opportunity to point out to the people of learning that the world, with its rapid march toward progress and advancement, must one day ascend the scale of benevolence, refinement, virtue, and good breeding, to the highest levels of perfection and the loftiest stations of moderation. Then, as the Holy Scriptures attest, will war be put away. Then, as it is stated in the divine promises, will the earth of potentialities reveal its treasures and mysteries. The character of the people will change; the customs of the world's inhabitants will be reformed. They will exchange their malice for love, their estrangement for affection, their harshness for tenderness and amity. "And they shall beat their swords into plowshares, and their spears into pruning hooks: nation shall not lift up sword against nation, neither shall they learn war any more."[25]

Will not our descendants look back on us at that time with contempt and derision, just as we look back at the ancients? Will they not depict us as savages and barbarians, just as we depict our predecessors? Has the time not arrived for us to arise from our sleep, to shake off our paralysis, to come to our senses, and to meditate a little on where matters are taking us? Let us cast the burden of ignorant fanaticism from about our necks! Let us blot out from the pages of our hearts the lines of religious and sectarian rancor! Let us bring up our children with love and compassion instead of, as we have been used to, training them in animosity and malevolence! We should trace loving-kindness and fidelity upon their hearts, where before we inscribed aversion and loathing. We should recite for them the verses of love and harmony, after having exposed their ears to the strains of hatred and discord.

All the regions of the earth will then rejoice at the portents of joy and felicity. The gardens of this world will blossom with the roses of happiness and delight. We shall become the heirs of the Gospel's saying, "Blessed are the meek, for they shall inherit the earth," and "Blessed are the peace-makers."[26] We shall be the confirmations of the Qur'án verse, "That is the Last Abode; We appoint it for those who desire not exorbitance in the earth, nor corruption."[27]

These hoary hatreds will never fade from our hearts until the leaders of the various religious communities show respect to one another. None of them must speak of another save with the tongue of courtesy. No scholar must criticize another of a different religious persuasion save with the utmost deference.

Every scholar may be criticized; indeed, criticism is a sign of advancement. But criticism differs from vituperation. The effort to enlighten and to be enlightened is quite another matter from abuse and invective. Should not a Christian, for instance, show respect for the statements and essays of the Muslim leaders; and the Muslim for the books and compositions of the Christian notables; and the Sunní for the eminent Shí'ís; and the Shí'í for the Sunní leaders? Only thus can these ancient antipathies be eradicated, and the filth of these blameworthy morals be cleansed. Only then will the flowers of bliss and good cheer blossom in the hearts, instead of the thorns of estrangement. Only then will they inherit the paradise of true humanity in the presence of the ever-forgiving Lord.

No treatise or essay in recent days has given me nearly so much pleasure as a piece written by the erudite writer Gád 'Íd, a refined young man of the

Christian community who was graduated from Syrian schools. He wrote a reply to the owner of the newspaper *Thamarát al-Funún*, which is printed in Beirut, concerning the main issue in the debate that took place between M. Hanotaux, the former French minister of foreign affairs, and one of the learned scholars of Islam in Egypt.[28] Newspaper owners in Egypt disagreed on this question, and each faction arose to aid its leader. Words multiplied, argument and wrangling intensified, until the affair recently led to the demand for a debate.

A brief summary of what occurred between the two sides is as follows: M. Hanotaux wrote a series of articles in the Parisian newspaper *Le Journal* on the Islamic religion and the way in which the French government should take it into account when dealing with its Muslim subjects in Tunisia, Algeria, and other countries to the west. Among the things Hanotaux wrote was that the Islamic religion is based on the remnants of the ancient Semitic religion and is founded on those sick and barren beliefs. He claimed-that it is a religion that leads to decline and decadence and produces lassitude and langour. This is owing to its belief in the unity of a God purified and sanctified from all that is related to the body or to bodily things. There is, he said, no link between Him and creation save that of blind worship and absolute submission to a predestined fate.

This is in contrast, he continued, to Christianity, which produces energy, combativeness, progress, advancement, and so on—including the highest imaginable human perfections and the most advanced level of humanity. It is, he stated, based on the Aryan religion, which was that of the ancient Greeks, who used to liken God to man in his characteristics and actions. He argued that this belief would necessarily make it possible for human beings to draw closer to the divine Essence, until man will be counted among the ranks of the gods of heaven.

He then proceeded to discuss how the French government should deal with its Muslim subjects. He lamented that it has failed to pursue a well-defined course with these unfortunate people—either of severity and regression or gentleness and flexibility. For the politicians and leaders of thought among them have differed over this issue. Kimon and his like judged that Muslims should be treated with severity and harshness.* They believed Islam to be a bitter enemy of Christianity because of the secondary differences they found between the laws of the two religions. Kimon said in his book *La Pathologie de l'Islam* that the Muḥammadan religion is a leprosy which has spread among the people, and he attacked it vigorously. He went on to say that Islam is an epidemic disease, a mass paralysis, a confused madness that plunges a man into a lethargic torpor and only arouses him from it to shed blood, or to devote himself to addictive liquors, or to defiantly commit abominations. Muḥammad's tomb in Mecca,† he asserted, is nothing but an electric pole that transmits insanity to the heads of the Muslims and compels them to manifest symptoms of epilepsy, mental stupor, and the constant, compulsive recitation of the word *Alláh*. It inclines them to habits that turn them toward their primitive natures, such as

*D. Kimon (b. 1860) was an obscure French polemicist and proponent of Aryan racial superiority. The book referred to here is *La Pathologie de l'Islam et les moyens de le détruire* [The pathology of Islam and the means to destroy it] (Paris: by the author, 1897).

†Muḥammad's tomb is actually in Medina.

an aversion to pork, wine, and music. It produces in them a spiritual lunacy, melancholia, and a sequence of acts that derives from cruel and licentious thoughts and absorption in delectations. Kimon then concluded that one-fifth of all Muslims should be wiped out and the rest sentenced to hard labor. He advocated the destruction of the Kaaba and the removal of Muḥammad's mausoleum to the Louvre Museum.

On the other hand, M. Hanotaux continued, some French thinkers have maintained that Islam and its civilization are tied to the Christian religion and to Christian civilization by the bonds of brotherhood and friendship. Some have even gone to extremes and considered Islam to be more advanced in its principles and more sublime in its glory than Christianity. The erudite priest and renowned orator Hyacinthe Loyson has judged that Islam is an improved and modified form of Christianity. He has advised Christians who are groping for their lost religiosity to seek the help of Islam in finding the object of their quest. Others have suggested that Islam deserves respect because it serves as a bridge whereby idolatrous Africans can move away from their paganism toward Christianity.

After M. Hanotaux reported these differing statements and conflicting views, he requested that the leaders of the French government and the leading politicians come to some agreement. He asked that they choose an appropriate principle and an ideal course somewhere between these contradictory opinions on how to treat the huge Muslim community that comprises the inhabitants of half the African continent. Only thus, he said, could a good result be attained and the great French Republic be safeguarded. When Hanotaux published his essay, it reached Egypt and was printed in translation in the *al-Mu'ayyad* newspaper. It aroused the emotions of the Egyptians, since it touched upon the honor of Islam.

The above-mentioned religious leader [Muḥammad 'Abduh] wrote a refutation of this article which was highly succinct, such as has no peer among the writings of contemporary Muslim scholars in the perfection of its exposition, the strength of its proofs, the fluency of its words, and the beauty of its argument. When the owner of *al-Mu'ayyad*[29] printed this rebuttal in his newspaper, the erudite received it with the utmost delight, their souls exulted, and their breasts were filled with joy. Then a group of Frenchmen undertook to raise objections to this rebuttal. Foremost among them was the owner of the famous daily *al-Ahrám*. He wrote a series of pieces: sometimes he refuted the owner of *al-Mu'ayyad*, and sometimes he objected to the contents of S͟hayk͟h Muḥammad 'Abduh's essays. Among the things he wrote concerning this subject was that *al-Mu'ayyad*'s editor corrupted Hanotaux's text by mistranslating it so as to distort its author's intentions.

The affair spread and became famous, and news of this dispute reached beyond Egypt to Syria. The articles of both parties were distributed there, and the owner of the daily *Thamarát al-Funún* asked Gád 'Íd about the reality of these issues, especially the matter of mistranslation. Had the owner of *al-Mu'ayyad* really corrupted the translation of Hanotaux's article, or was it an exact rendering? This refined and cultured gentleman, in spite of his youth and his steadfast, upright adherence to Christianity, penned a treatise responding to those questions with the greatest fairness and moderation. I have never before seen a man, under such conditions, act so equitably and respectfully toward someone who is not of his own religion. I would like to quote his very words, that they may serve as an adornment to this book and a radiant lamp to the possessors of insight:

> Sir: I have often perused the essay in French by M. Hanotaux which has agitated minds and pens, and I can say that the translation offered by *al-Mu'ayyad* is not erroneous. However, Hanotaux was not satisfied simply to report the words of Kimon; he openly derided his thoughts and the very extremist solution he proposed to the Islamic question. The translator of Hanotaux's essay in *al-Mu'ayyad* has completely preserved the sense of the original, remaining content to put question marks and dots indicating disavowal. However, readers of Arabic are not used to these punctuation marks used by Europeans, and do not understand their significance. For this reason, their meaning was obscured and many thought that Hanotaux was indicating his approval of Kimon's statements. But even so, Hanotaux resumed his discussion after quoting Kimon and returned once more to the subject of Islam. He declared himself innocent of the charges made against it and stated his sympathy and respect for Islam and Muslims. His essay was translated by *al-Mu'ayyad* and also later by *al-Ahrám*. Then the journal *al-Liwá'* entered the arena of dispute, and the French editor of *al-Ahrám* was annoyed at this. Muṣṭafá Bey Kámil invited him to a debate.[30] After this, various statements were made; Taqlá Pá<u>sh</u>á challenged the owner of *al-Liwá'*. The two parties heaped abuse on one another, and their helpers and disciples took sides.
>
> Sir: Had *al-Mu'ayyad* and *al-Liwá'* contented

themselves with printing what that great religious leader [Muḥammad 'Abduh] wrote, they would have truly served Islam. For truth is felled when one endeavors to make it known through curses and imprecations. Moreover, it was not only on the Muslims that S͟hayk͟h Muḥammad 'Abduh's rebuttal made such a great impression. Indeed, many eminent Christians referred to it often and gave it a noble place. I do not exaggerate when I say to you that I read it more than twenty times.

The religion of Islam is one of noble-mindedness, valor, freedom, and pure civilization. However, Kimon and his like have only learned of things contrary to the spirit of Islam and Muslims, and remote from their beliefs, manners, and morals. European authors do not control their emotions in their enthusiasm. Many of them have even written calumnies about the Lord Christ, the chastity of his mother, and the honor of his disciples. A large number of them have occupied themselves with assailing great and righteous persons, making scandalous pronouncements about them such as have caused the limbs of courtesy and virtue to quake. When a people has reached this degree of extremism and conceit, is it fitting to translate their statements and broadcast their absurdities for all to see, thereby stirring up concealed hatreds?

Your religion dawned with its brilliant light upon darkened visions and illumined them. It came to fettered minds, guided them, and broke their bonds. It appeared to sleeping souls, awakened them, and corrected their wrongs. I earnestly adjure you by this religion to take up your pen and signal with it a praiseworthy goal: this is to arouse the aspirations of the leading Muslim writers to defend Islam in the ways that Islam itself desires. These ways are not mysterious to the eminent Muslims who have inculcated in their hearts a love of amity, meekness, and peace. The true defense of Islam is to incite the community to acquire sublime virtues in honoring its neighbors and supporting their rights, and to treat God's servants with equality, justice, and faithfulness.

Many who have never had the honor of personally encountering Islam are manifestly in error in their thoughts and suppositions about Islam and about Muslims. But the effects of their errors can be eradicated only by decisive and outstanding proofs that can establish for them that Islam is a religion of complete freedom, true compassion, real sagacity; and by the preservation of good breeding, noble morals, honor, sincerity, and loyalty.

My good sir: Do you think that Kimon would have spit this filth from his mouth had he ever read even one chapter embroidered by the fingers of 'Alí ibn Abí Ṭálib? Do you think he would have dared to propose his dreadful solution to the Islamic question had he ever heard of the forbearance and wisdom of the two 'Umars, the nobility of ibn Zá'idah, the justice of Harún ar-Ras͟híd, or the generosity of the Barmakids?* Do you think he would have set pen to paper if he had known

*The two 'Umars are 'Umar ibn al-K͟haṭṭáb (r. 644–656 A.D.), the second "rightly guided" caliph for the Sunnís, and 'Umar ibn 'Abdu'l-'Azíz (r. 717–720 A.D.), the Umayyid king known for his unusual piety. Harun ar-Rashíd (r. 786–809 A.D.) was the caliph of the 'Abbásid Empire during its golden age. The Barmakid family had been Buddhist priests at Balkh before converting to Islam. They produced several important bureaucrats and viziers for the 'Abbásid dynasty (from 750 A.D.). They were known for their munificence and power but fell suddenly from favor in 803 A.D.

that even the most despicable man among the Muslims would shed the last drop of his blood to defend the honor and nobility or someone who had sought refuge with him, if that person should ask him for protection?

However deluded and misled Kimon and his like might be, after truly knowing Islam they would only be able to praise it and take pride in its virtues.

I wish from the depths of my heart to add my voice to those that have affirmed the truth, and I counsel the eminent Muslims to take a seemly course in their arguments to overcome the iniquity of their assailants. May God aid you in this regard! However, some of the ignorant among them desire to bring the truth low by their meddling in the crafts of writing and composition. I do not conceal anything from you. The pens that have written after the moderate and masterful refutation by Shaykh Muḥammad 'Abduh have produced nothing of value, but have rather obscured, or nearly obscured, the truth, which is on your side. They have provoked a furor with which the reasonable ones among the Islamic community are not pleased. Peace.

Cairo
9 June 1900
Gád 'Íd

Here we shall close this essay. We beseech God to confirm you and us under all conditions. He is, verily, the Confirmer, the Most High. This was completed by the pen of Abu'l-Faḍl Gulpáygání of Iran, the son of Muḥammad Riḍá, on 20 Ṣafar 1318 A.H. [1900 A.D.].

Part IV

An Essay on the Meaning of Miracles and the Degree to Which Each Type Constitutes a Proof

ABRAHAM AMID THE FLAMES
from the Anthology of Iskandár Sulṭán. S̲h̲iráz, 1410. Gulbenkian Foundation, Lisbon.

On the Two Kinds of Signs

EVERYONE AGREES that it is necessary for the Manifestations of the Cause of God and the promulgators of His law to possess some special attribute, a recognizable sign to distinguish them and to set them apart from others. This sign serves as witness and evidence for them and is a proof of their truth. From the time of the earliest peoples until the time of the Apostle of God, Muḥammad, this distinguishing characteristic was called *al-áyah,* a word meaning "sign." Whenever anyone claimed to be a messenger of God, they used to ask him for a sign that might guide them to recognize the truth of his words and might establish the soundness of his claims.

Thus, in the Gospel of Matthew (chapter 12) it is mentioned that the scribes and Pharisees asked Jesus to produce a sign for them. "He replied, 'An evil and adulterous generation seeks for a sign; but no sign shall be given to it except the sign of the prophet Jonah.'"[1] In the sixteenth chapter of the same book, it is reported that the Pharisees and Sadducees came to him to test him and asked him to show them a sign from heaven. "He answered them, 'When it is evening, you say, "It will be fair weather; for the sky is red." And in the morning, "It will be stormy today, for the sky is red and threatening." You know how to interpret the appearance of the sky, but you cannot interpret the signs of the times. An evil and adulterous generation seeks for a sign, but no sign shall be given to it except the sign of Jonah.' So he left them and departed.''[2] The meaning of all this is that the learned men of the Jews demanded from him as a test that he work a miracle for them. We shall explain his answer below.

The Holy Qur'án reports that the Quraysh tribe and others said, ''Now therefore let him bring us a sign, even as the ancient ones.'' And also, ''Why does he not bring us a sign from his Lord?''[3] There are many such verses, which establish that such terms as ''miracle,'' ''preternatural event,'' ''grace,'' and so forth, are words newly coined by modern men, and that there was no mention of them among ancient peoples.

After the spread of the religion of Jesus and the establishment of his Word, the learned among the Christians changed the term ''sign'' to ''wonder.'' Perhaps this latter word is taken from the terminology of the ''Sabian'' religion, which was the religion of the peoples of Europe, Africa, and Asia (excluding the Indians and Chinese) before the appearance of Moses, Jesus, and Muḥammad.*

Some of the ancient Egyptian records preserved in the famed Cairo Museum, which have been translated during my stay in Egypt, indicate that in Pharaonic times Egyptians used to refer to preternatural phenomena as ''wonders.'' As for the learned among Muslims —that is, the early ones—they understood that God

*In the Qur'án, the ''Sabians'' probably refers to the Mandaeans, a Judeo-Christian sect in Mesopotamia which put special emphasis on John the Baptist and on baptism as a rite. Later, a pagan group which practiced a gnostic mystery religion at Ḥarrán took the name ''Sabians'' and became renowned in the Muslim world. Mírzá Abu'l-Faḍl has therefore, used the word generally to refer to all non-Judaic and non-Indic religions of antiquity. His point here is that the idea of Jesus as a miracle-worker probably derived from these pagan traditions, rather than from Judaism.

had commanded the Prophet to present the Qur'án as a proof for the soundness of his claims. Every sentence of the Holy Book was called a "sign" whenever the people would demand from him some other sign. The early scholars saw that the various "signs" differed in their meanings and influence, and so they divided them into two categories, as is clear from their commentaries.

The first category consists of "signs" of the Book, which is to say, divine revelation. These refer to the truths and the meanings revealed through the medium of the Faithful Spirit to the hearts of the prophets and messengers. These meanings then appeared in the form of words spoken by their tongues and became manifest in language expressed from their lips.

According to the Shí'ís, both these meanings and the words that express them are created by God. They hold that these revealed meanings are divine, innate knowledge which is not learned. The words expressing them are "the speech of God," and the speech of no one else. Speech, as specialists in this area know, is only a group of invented words deriving from phonemes. These phonemes themselves, as scientists and philosophers have established, are only waves of air pressured between something striking and something struck. These is no other kind of speech, nor does it make sense to talk of "mental speech."

The Sunnís hold that the revealed meanings are preexistent, and that they are attributes of God. They refer to them as the "preexistent speech." For them, the fact that the words are created does not negate the preexistence of their meanings—which they call "mental speech"—any more than the mortality and createdness of bodies negates the permanence and eternality of souls. For these words are but a framework for mental speech which, in actuality, is the preexistent, subsisting reality of God's essence. These are the divine "signs" and celestial words referred to in the verses of the Qur'án.

The speech of the creature is distinguished from the speech of the Creator by certain signs and tokens. The first sign is the most manifest and the greatest: the speech itself ascribes and imputes itself to God, as it is mentioned in the Holy Qur'án: "Nor does he speak out of caprice. This is naught but a revelation revealed."[4] If this were a lie or invention, it would pass away by itself and be proven false by its own essence. God has promised, in His ancient wisdom and age-old Faith, to assure the destruction of whoso falsely attributes words to Him and to erase whatever is imputed to Him without His permission. What is false is ephemeral and cannot survive, nor will the designs of a lying inventor succeed.

The second sign is that the Book of God vanquish its opposers, conquer those who struggle against it, and prove able to bring about the downfall of its foes.

The third sign is that these words prove effective in founding a religious community, creating a lasting religious law with effective judgments, and firmly establishing the Word. This sign would only be reasonable, and can only appear, when the speech includes a new set of religious laws, and new traditions and ordinances. Otherwise, legislation is left to the previous messenger, and the old scriptures retain their effect and influence. These latter two signs are vouched for by the holy verse revealed in the perspicuous Book: "God was desiring to verify the truth by His words, and to cut off the unbelievers to the last remnant."[5]

God's speech has other signs, such as its effects on personal affairs, its elucidation of the mysteries reposited in past Holy Scriptures, its obvious linguistic virtues, and so forth. Specialists in this area know all these. We have devoted only a few pages to mentioning them, in an attempt to be brief and owing to a lack of opportunity to compete in this arena. What we have said will suffice for the insightful.

The second category consists of verses that were suggested by the people. These are acts that are normally impossible, but which the community, or some among it, propose to one who claims the station of a prophet or messenger. They make their belief in him dependent on his ability to perform them, and they test him by means of such proposals. These include such matters as inducing stones to speak and trees to obey one's command, causing springs and rivers to flow, raising the dead to life, transforming a staff into serpent, parting the sea with a staff, and so on. There is no end to such things, nor can anyone ever get his fill of them, or have his thirst for them quenched. As is apparent in the noble Qur'án and the Holy Gospel, one of the characteristics of such proposed signs is that they lead to perdition and result in destruction. They fail to bring certainty or guidance to those with discernment, and only the dissolute and evil request or suggest them. We shall clarify the reasons for this to the people of insight.

In the Middle Ages, the terms "miracle" and "preternatural event" were metaphorically applied to the meaning properly conveyed by the word "sign," because no one in those times could bring forth their like, and since they interrupt the ordinary course of events to which people are accustomed. Later, these words took on a literal sense secondarily.

Still later thinkers divided miracles into other categories. They said that if a deed that broke the natural order was performed by someone before he was given a prophetic mission, this should be called a great exertion.[6] If it was performed after he received his mission, in conjunction with a challenge to or reproach of the people, it should be called a miracle. Miracles were not imputed to anyone but prophets. If the special deed appeared from a man who made no challenge or claim, and revealed no divine law or reproach, it was called a grace. Only saints were said to have graces. If the extraordinary feat was accomplished by a satanic, wicked person, it was termed sorcery or enchantment. This is what is said of the ancient sorcerers.

Anyone who knows the facts can recognize the degree to which these terms are inane, and how far those who employ them are from a knowledge of the true meaning of the revealed verses and sayings. With these terms the truth of the All-Merciful's saying becomes apparent: "They are naught but names that you and your fathers have named; God has sent down no authority touching them."[7] However, it is not permitted for scholars to harass the people concerning the terms they employ or to quarrel with them over their language. It has been said, "Do not quarrel over words." Therefore, let us leave behind the people and their views and speak of the degree to which miracles constitute evidence and extraordinary events are a proof of anything.

It is obvious that any evidence or proof must be related to the thing for which the evidence or proof is presented. Otherwise, it cannot be considered proof or evidence—no matter how astonishing or amazing. For instance, let us say someone claims to be a physician, learned in the arts of preserving health and treating ailments. Let us further say that he presents as proof of the soundness of this claim his ability to fly. Now, even should he do this, his flight does not necessarily constitute evidence that he is a physician, though it would certainly be an amazing and astonishing feat. For flight is not among the attributes of the skill in question: there is no link between it and the science of medicine. Rather, preserving health and releasing the ailing from diseases are the attributes of this skill and constitute evidence related to the soundness of this claim and the truth of this assertion.

The American Professor Cornelius van Dyck, in the eighth chapter of his book on logic, *Engraving on Stone*,[8] says, "Insofar as man is subject to error in matters of reason, it is appropriate for him to seek the aid of a lawful instrument that will serve to protect him from error and to guide him to the truth. Thus will he avoid regarding something as a cause when it is not, or considering something an effect when it is not. He will avoid building on a rotten foundation and will not count as a proof that which is no proof." And Imám al-G͟hazálí said, "Let us suppose someone says, 'Four is greater than ten, and I shall demonstrate this by transforming this staff into a serpent.' Let us say he does so, and the staff becomes a serpent. I would be astonished at the artifice of the one who did it. But I would retain my certitude that four is less than ten. . . ."[9] The point is that there is no relation between the proof and the thing proved, and therefore it is not counted as a proof.

Once one has understood this premise, one can see with the utmost ease that there is no relation between the claim to be a messenger of God and the power to perform actions which are normally impossible. For the claim to be a messenger in itself does not require that the one who makes it must have the power to perform things that pertain to the one who sent him. For instance, let us say a man claimed that he was sent by a king to carry out a judgment or to announce some edict or prohibition. His claim to be a messenger does not itself necessitate or require that the messenger be able to do whatever the king could do, or that he possess the same royal characteristics, such as being able to lead soldiers, conquer fortresses, kill persons, appoint ministers, dismiss commanders, and so forth. Moreover, even if the messenger were capable of some of these actions, he would not perform any of them just because they were suggested to him or demanded of him, since they are irrelevant and unconnected to his claim.

For instance, if a man claimed to have been appointed governor of the Punjab in India by the queen of England, and some people opposed him, demanding from him a proof of the soundness of his assertion, he would certainly cite the orders of the queen and the letter she gave him establishing his appointment and proving his office. Let us suppose that skeptics refused to submit to the authority of his letter and paid no attention to his documents on the grounds that anyone can forge such papers. Let us further suppose that they demanded he perform some sign associated with kingship or some deed appropriate to a governor, such as imprisoning people, killing certain persons, or appointing and dismissing officials from their posts, as is expected from viceroys and governors, so that they might submit to his proof and obey his authority. It is obvious that he would not deign to respond to their demands, nor would he allow them to fulfill their hopes. He would only cite the queen's letter and hold fast to the decree of the ruler of the realm—even though he might be capable of performing what they requested, such as appointing, dismissing, imprisoning, and killing. For these matters have times, circumstances, requirements, and personnel which he may not alter on his own authority or change by himself.

This is the secret of God's saying, "It was not for any Messengers to bring a sign but by God's leave."[10] For sending messengers and ordaining religious laws, in the world of the spirit, resembles the assignment of princes, the appointment of governors, and the legislation of manmade civil laws in this world.

From what we have established, it is quite clear that this statement of God in the Surah of the Cattle: "Say: 'I do not say to you, "I possess the treasuries of God"; I know not the unseen. And I say not to you, "I am an angel"; I only follow what is revealed to me.' Say: 'Are the blind and the seeing man equal? Will you not reflect?'"[11] is only meant to present rational evidence and clear proof that the claim to be a messenger of God neither requires nor demands the power to perform things normally impossible. Should someone, for instance, assert that he knows all unseen things, a test of his knowldge of a particular unseen event would be related to his claim. For this particular unseen event is one of the individual elements that make up the totality of a knowledge of all unseen things, which is what is claimed. Between these two there is a link of universality and particularity, and the necessity that the truth of the whole be applicable to the parts. Or, to take another example, should someone announce that he controls the treasuries of heaven and earth, it would be relevant to test this assertion by asking that he produce some particular treasure, for the reason we stated above: this is one of the particulars making up the totality. It is necessary that the whole be applicable to the parts, and that its truth be related to them.

As for being a messenger of God, this is not made

up of those proposed impossible feats, nor is it a form abstracted from such things. There exists between the two, therefore, not the slightest connection. However, the intent of the blessed verse we have quoted was not to deny any power, but rather to reject any connection between the claim to be a messenger and the power to perform extraordinary exploits. This is also the case with the verse revealed in the Surah of the Night Journey: "They say: 'We will not believe thee till thou makest a spring to gush forth from the earth for us, or till thou possessest a garden of palms and vines, and thou makest rivers to gush forth abundantly all amongst it, or till thou makest heaven to fall, as thou assertest, on us in fragments, or thou bringest God and the angels as a surety, or till thou possessest a house of gold ornament, or till thou goest up into heaven; and we will not believe thy ascension till thou bringest down to us a book that we may read.' Say: 'Glory be to my Lord! Am I aught but a mortal, a Messenger?'"[12]

What God ordered the Prophet to say in reply to these suggestions of the people is itself a clear statement that the claim to be a messenger does not necessitate the power to carry out such suggestions. That is, the Prophet's words, "Glory be to my Lord! Am I aught but a mortal, a Messenger?" deny that there is any link or relation between his station as messenger and the ability to perform what was suggested. However, they do not deny the ability itself. For it is rationally tenable that the Prophet was able to perform these things, but that his claim to be a messenger did not require him to show them forth. In the same way, a governor is capable of appointing some individuals and removing others, however, he does not do so in order to establish that he is governor. He does these things only when the law permits and when particular circumstances and times call for them.

This has been established, and the connection between the Book and the claim to be a messenger has also been demonstrated. We, therefore, hold that the signs of the Book (that is, divine revelation) possess obvious virtues over those proposed signs, which are called miracles and wonders, from several points of view. The first virtue is that the Book presents primary evidence for the truth of the claim [to give divine revelation]. This is owing to the guidance that has been reposited herein, for the sake of which the messengers have been sent and the prophets given their missions. This guidance directly pertains to the characteristics of the action concerned, in contrast to the other miracles. For such miracles would constitute a warning of perdition should they be performed after the people propose them, or they would give secondary supporting evidence for the claim if performed without being suggested. This is because they are not characteristics of the action concerned: there is no relation between them and being a prophet or messenger, as has been pointed out at length above.

The learned judge Averroes of Spain said in his book, *Exposition on Methods of Evidence Concerning the Doctrines of the Community,* in regard to this matter, "Given all this, he [Muḥammad] excelled the other prophets [in the universality of his divine legislation]. For he surpassed them in revelation, whereby a prophet merits the name 'prophet.' Therefore he said, drawing attention to this quality for which God had singled him out, 'All prophets without exception have been given verses, in the like of which all men have believed. What I was given was only revelation, and I hope to follow it more than anyone else on the Resurrection Day.' If all this is as we have described it, it will be clear to you that the evidence the Qur'án represents for his prophethood—may the peace and blessings of God be upon him—differs from the evidence the transformation of his staff into a serpent gives for the prophethood of Moses (upon whom be peace), or which the raising of the dead to life and the curing of the blind and the lepers gives for the prophethood of Jesus (upon whom be peace). These, though they might be acts that are performed only by prophets, and though they might prove convincing to the masses, do not present decisive evidence in and of themselves, since they are not among the actions pertaining to the quality whereby a prophet is called a prophet. As for the Qur'án, it gives evidence for this quality in the same way that the ability to cure is evidence that one is a physician."[13]

The holy verse that was revealed in the Surah of the Spider alludes to this point, which has been widely ignored: "They say, 'Why have signs not been sent down upon him from his Lord?' Say: 'The signs are only with God, and I am only a plain warner.' What, is it not sufficient to them that We have sent down upon thee the Book that is recited to them? Surely in that is a mercy, and a reminder to a people who believe."[14]

This verse points clearly and unambiguously to some of the matters we have referred to in this essay. The first is that the Prophet Muḥammad never sought to establish the authenticity of his station as a messenger of God by miracles. The people even called out in public, asking why, if Muḥammad were a real prophet and a true messenger, God did not endow him with miracles. Second, the performance of miracles is solely a matter for God. Its import is that they are not matters for prophets, since the business of a prophet is simply to warn. Third, the Book constitutes sufficient evidence and ample proof for the soundness of his claims and the truth of his statements. The reasons for this are that in this Book alone has God reposited the mercy, guidance, commemoration, and exhortation by reason of which the messengers were sent and religious laws ordained—and more, for the sake of which branches of knowledge were founded and schools established. For they are a stairway to civilization, a ladder for ascent to the highest levels of humanity, and plumage for the mind's flight into the spacious worlds of spirituality.

The second virtue of the Book over other signs is that the Book remains eternally, in contrast to miracles, and particularly to suggested ones, which are evanescent and ephemeral.

The third virtue is that the Book is easy to acquire and may be sent to every land, so that every seeker may peruse it and every pilgrim may obtain it. This stands in contrast to other miracles which concern only those present to see them and exclude those who are absent. For these two latter reasons (that is, permanence and ease of acquisition), the Book has been called "the universal proof," since it can be sent to the farthest reaches of civilization and will last until the end of the dispensation. Even supposing that Jesus raised the dead, healed lepers, and gave speech to the mute, or that our lord the Prophet split the moon, caused the stones to speak, and that the stars and trees obeyed him—how can these things compare with the Gospel and the Qur'án, and the light and proof God has reposited therein? The Book is read in every assembly and perused in every country. All with vision see it, all with ears hear it, all who are prepared take heed from it. All people benefit from it, so that the proof may be universal and the evidence complete, until the preordained term expires and realities attain their highest potential and then begin preparations for their appearance in a new beginning.

The fourth virtue is that true knowledge and the

Holy Book are the two most noble things, and so may constitute proof for the noblest of men. This question is fundamental: it is natural and instinctive. It does not require a great deal of explanation, since there is no virtue higher than knowledge and insight. It is well known that a man's honor lies in his knowledge, and that the repository of all knowledge is the Holy Book. This is the meaning of God's verse, "Say: 'Are the blind and the seeing equal? Will you not reflect?'" and the verse, "Say: Are they equal—those who know and those who know not?"[15]

This is also referred to in the beginning of the section on the Proof in the book *al-Káfí,* where Abú 'Abdi'lláh Ja'far aṣ-Ṣádiq, one of the imams of the House of the Prophet, is quoted. When a skeptic asked him, "How do you establish the truth of the prophets?" he replied: "We have established that we have a Creator and Maker who is exalted above us and all that was created. This Maker is wise and elevated such that it is impossible for his creatures to see Him or touch Him, and such that the former cannot come into contact with the latter, nor can they reason with one another. It is therefore necessary that He send envoys to His creation who will tell His people and servants of Him, and who will direct them to that wherein they may find benefit, advantage, and continued life. Without this they shall be extinguished. Thus are vindicated those who enjoin good and prohibit evil among the people on behalf of the All-Wise, the All-Knowing, and who speak forth of Him. These are the prophets and His chosen ones, sages trained in wisdom, those sent forth, those who—despite sharing with the people the quality of being created and composed—are free from any of their limitations. These are confirmed with wisdom by the All-Knowing, the All-Wise. This has been established in every age and time, that messengers and prophets have brought evidence and proofs so that God's earth might not lack a Proof, and there might be with him a knowledge that will demonstrate the truth of his sayings and the possibility of his justice."[16] In this noble saying can be discerned the marks of successorship and the legacy of the prophets and messengers. For the envoys of God have been granted a superiority to the rest of the creation in knowledge and wisdom, quite apart from the miracles and extraordinary events to which the people hold.

The fifth virtue is that seeking miracles and proposing signs contradicts the whole purpose of sending prophets and messengers with the path of rectitude. For the greatest benefit, and mightiest cause, for the dispatch of messengers and the establishment of divine laws is to test the servants, weigh their hearts, and purify their spirits. Thus are the wicked distinguished from the good, the profligate from the virtuous, the infidel from the faithful, and the doubter from the certain. Their true natures are thus tested and their true conditions made plain. Before the appearance of the prophet and the revelation of his verses, the land of being and the trees of the heart are quiet, calm, still, and motionless. Then, when God releases the water of revelation from on high, the rain of holy verses pours down from the clouds of grace: all the earth shakes, and every tree grows, sprouts, reaches great height, and puts forth leaves and blossoms. Then concealed realities are manifest, and hidden signs appear. The excellent is distinguished from the spoiled, the sound from the corrupt, and the good from the wicked. Thus is the test completed and the process of purification achieved, as we were clearly and specifically promised in the first scriptures.

JONAH CAST UP BY A GREAT FISH
Rashíd ad-Dín. Persian painting, c. 1400. The Metropolitan Museum of Art, Bequest of Joseph Pulitzer, 1933. [33.113]

The Unhealthy Effect of Demanding Signs

As for demanding extraordinary signs of prophets and proposing miracles, this is a test and a trial of the prophets themselves. Indeed, this is nothing more than an attempt by the people to prove them and to chasten them. This is, as we pointed out above, contradictory to the benefit of sending prophets and messengers. Indeed, it represents haughtiness toward God, hostility to His will, opposition to His pleasure, and attack on His wisdom. This, as we said before, presages perdition and degradation and inevitably leads to depravity and ruin. Call to mind God's saying, "And We do not send the signs, except to inspire fear." That is also the intent of the Old Testament verse, "You shall not put the Lord your God to a test," and of the saying in the Gospel, "An evil and adulterous generation seeks for a sign."[17]

Anyone who examines the various classes of people at the time of a prophet's appearance, and the beginning of a new religion will see that the highest rank of believers, such as the disciples of Jesus and the companions of Muḥammad, did not test the Manifestations of the Cause of God. They never proposed signs for them to perform but, rather, unhesitatingly submitted themselves to the radiance of their authority, the brilliance of their proof, the recitation of their verses, and the influence of their word. They believed and attained certitude without doubting or growing suspicious. They arose by virtue of that power beyond which there is no other, to ensure the victory of the religion of God, to promulgate His Cause, to spread His Word, and to exalt His mention. They led nations out of darkness into light, transformed peoples from pagans into believers in one God, and guided them from the adoration of idols to the worship of the All-Merciful. They left behind them glorious exploits and splendid deeds that no person of insight will doubt.

As for those who demanded miracles, proposed signs, and tried their messengers with superstitions, they were tested before they could test others, and they were subjected to trials even as they sought to try others. They did not believe and did not obey. They clung to their unbelief and lingered in their state of transgression until they perished with other ancient peoples. Only their stories survive as an example to others. These are a few of the virtues of the Holy Book and reasons that it is to be preferred to other miracles, whether proposed or otherwise. We have recited them to you to the extent that our Lord has graced us with the clouds of His kindness and has bestowed upon us from the oceans of His knowledge.

From all this we can discern the reason that our lord Jesus avoided responding to the Jews when they proposed signs to him and demanded miracles of him, as we have quoted from the twelfth and sixteenth chapters of Matthew. There are many such examples in other places. As for the Holy Qur'án, therein are many unambiguous verses on the refusal to produce miracles and the evil end of those who demand signs. We cannot cite all of them in this concise essay, but we will quote some of them for those of sound discrimination, hearing ears, and understanding hearts. Thus might they understand the meaning of these verses and become aware of the grave consequences of proposing miracles and the unhealthy effect of demanding signs.

Among these is God's saying in the Surah of the Night Journey, "We refrain from sending signs only because the former generations treated them as false. We brought the Thamúd* the She-Camel to open their eyes, but they did her wrong. And We do not send signs, except to inspire fear."[18] Whoever contemplates this noble verse will see that it asserts openly, and in a way not susceptible to any figurative interpretation, that God refused to manifest miracles because the ancients denied their reality. They rejected the miracles of the prophets, so God destroyed them by their denial and obliterated them by their rejection. In the same way, the Thamúd transgressed against the She-Camel and denied this sign, so they were effaced and annihilated.

The reason for this is that God only sends signs as an omen of destruction or as a harbinger of devastation. His saying in the Surah of Cattle also points this out: "Say: 'I stand upon a clear sign from my Lord, and you have denied it. What you seek to hasten is not with me; the judgment is God's alone. He relates the truth, and He is the Best of deciders.' Say: 'If what you seek to hasten were with me, the matter between you and me would be decided; and God knows the evildoers very well.'"[19] It is obvious that what the unbelievers in Mecca beseeched the Prophet to hasten was the demonstration of a sign to them. This is the case with the appearance of every prophet and messenger, and of anyone who calls people to God.

*Thamúd was an ancient Arabian tribe which rejected Ṣáliḥ, the messenger God sent to them. See Bahá'u'lláh, *Kitáb-i-Íqán*, pp. 9–10, and Qur'án 11:61–62.

Whenever any messenger appears, the first thing the people suggest to him is that he perform a miracle. They do not stop to consider whether or not this would prove anything. And if the prophet declines to respond to their request, they insist on their demand and become obstinate in pursuing the request. This is demonstrated by the verse in the Surah of Cattle: "They have sworn by God the most earnest oaths that if a sign comes to them they will believe in it. Say: 'Signs are only with God.' What will make you realize that, when it comes, they will not believe? We shall turn about their hearts and their eyes, even as they failed to believe in it the first time; and We shall leave them wandering blindly in their insolence. Though We had sent down the angels to them, and the dead had spoken with them, had We gathered together against them every thing, face to face, yet they would not have believed, unless God willed; but most of them are ignorant."[20]

When the Prophet appeared, the eminent men among the Arabs engaged in disputes with him, as is known by both scholars and laymen. They took the mightiest oaths and swore with the greatest earnestness, saying: "'By God, the Living, the Preexistent!' and 'By God, the Truth, the Mighty!' If Muḥammad demonstrates a sign (that is, a miracle), we will believe in him." They repeated this oath and persisted in swearing. God responded to them that signs are with God. That is, He is capable of performing miracles; but should He do so, they would not believe in them because, afterwards, He would confuse their hearts and eyes and forsake them in their wandering and hesitation, so that their condition would be the same as before the miracle was requested. They will refuse to believe or to obey, just as they refused before the proof appeared. The reason for this is that, as we have said, miracles do not in themselves constitute evidence for being a messenger or prophet, and there is no relation between the claim to be a prophet and the power to perform things that are normally impossible.

However, save for the few whom God awakened by the spirit of vigilance and in whose hearts was kindled the lamp of watchfulness, all the people have been heedless of this point and have drowned in a sea of idle fancies passed down from a hoary age of ignorance. For this reason, they proposed miracles to their messengers without first considering and reflecting.

Let us suppose that a prophet had acceded to their request and demonstrated for them the demanded sign and the proposed miracle. The people would have instinctively become aware that it was not evidential or related to the prophet's claim, and so they would have rejected it and denied it, or attributed it to sorcery, legerdemain, or some other imaginary, groundless factor. At that point, perdition would inevitably have fallen upon them and chastisement would inevitably have been visited upon them. For they would have broken their oath, violated their word, and cast aside their covenants, just as had the unbelieving nations and the extinct peoples that passed away before them. That is why God, in the Qur'án, ascribed their lack of faith to the fact that their hearts and visions were changed, that is, their thoughts and views were turned around and the course of their perceptions and feelings altered.

Once God turned their hearts and minds to an awareness of this irrelevance and lack of proof, they would indubitably remain in their former state of doubt and uncertainty. For faith is only the reassurance of the heart, and no heart can be reassured except through a relevant proof. But there is no reasonable link between the claim to be a messenger of God and what they demanded. It was therefore fitting that God left them to their transgression, allowing them to hesitate and to wander astray. Thus, God explained to His noble Messenger that, even if he were to perform the most prodigious miracles and cause miraculous signs to appear—even the descent of angels to these people, the resurrection of the dead and their conversation with the living, and the gathering together of everything before the eyes of this blind nation—the unbelievers would not believe in it. In short, these miracles would not serve to guide them and would not deliver them from error.

For guidance depends on the will and volition of God. It is contingent on His permission and power, and not on the appearance of these signs, or on seeing these extraordinary proposals fulfilled. The reason for this is apparent to those of clear vision, for guidance and error depend on the tenderness or hardness, the light or the darkness, the purity or corruption that the heart has acquired in its early days and in its former religion. This is because, as we have established, all religions have been ordained by God. They are established and safeguarded, and they continue for a fixed period, a preordained term, by virtue of His Word. All of them are roads to the ultimate goal and doors to the highest heaven. To disregard them must lead to error; to follow them conveys guidance. No soul is punished save for what it has done while traveling this distant interval and this extended term. Your Lord is not an oppressor of His servants.

Another verse is: "We know that it grieves thee the things they say; yet it is not thee they reject, but it is the signs of God that the evildoers deny. Messengers indeed were rejected before thee, yet they endured rejection and harm patiently until Our succor came to them. No man can change the words of God; and there has already come to thee some tiding of the Envoys. And if their turning away is distressful to thee, why, if thou canst, seek out a hole in the earth, or a ladder in heaven, to bring them some sign. But had God willed, He would have gathered them to the guidance; so be not thou one of the ignorant."[21]

These noble verses were revealed when sorrows had encompassed the Messenger of God. Severe tribulations had overcome him, and he was harried by various groups who were constantly demanding miracles of him. They rejected and despised his verses, going so far as to call the words of the Qur'án lies, poetry, and legends of bygone peoples.

Some of them went to extremes in censuring and rejecting him, saying and calling out, "O God, if this indeed be the truth from Thee, then rain down upon us stones out of heaven or bring us a painful chastisement."[22] They demonstrated their total and complete rejection, having no doubt or hesitancy in their denial. God then revealed this verse to console His Prophet, showing that He knew the degree to which sorrows had overtaken him and anxieties overwhelmed him. He informed him that the transgressors do not reject the messenger of God; rather, in reality, they deny the verses of God. He thus implied that a rejection of the messenger was nothing compared to a denial of the sacred verses and opposition to the Holy Book. Therein is a severe danger and a fearful peril which is not concealed from those with penetrating vision and insight. No tyrant has ever rejected the Book, despised its verses, or denied these signs but that God has broken his back, blunted his sword, crushed his fangs, humiliated his successors, destroyed his helpmates, and obliterated all trace of him, so that he became a proverbial example to succeeding centuries and generations.

God reminded His Prophet of how the great prophets and virtuous chosen ones who preceded him were rejected and persecuted. They patiently bore the torments of affliction and the anguish of trials until the succor of God came to them, and they vanquished the enemies of God. He had to be patient as they were patient; he had to bear suffering as they had. For the word of God is not subject to alteration, nor does God change the way He sends messengers and ordains religious laws. So God recounted to the Prophet stories of the bygone peoples and tales of others who went before, so that he might be informed of his Cause, confident of his Lord, and certain of his triumph and victory.

Then He departed from a stance of consolation and sympathy to one of severity and scolding. He spoke words to the effect that, "If you find it difficult to bear patiently the rejection of the unbelievers and the ridicule of the wicked, then seek out, if you can, a hole in the earth or a ladder to the sky. Perhaps you will find a miracle or bring them a sign that will silence their rejection of you and cause them to cease quarreling with you." Then He informed the noble Messenger that God, should He will, could cause them to agree upon His guidance and could compel them all to submit to His holy law. Is not He capable of guiding all, He who guided the Arab nobles and the chiefs of their tribes to the path of faith and the gift of obedience—in spite of their notorious fanaticism and Arab pride, their bedouin arrogance and ignorant obstinacy? Is not He able to unite the Arabs in faith and cause them to forsake their enmity and feuding—He who transformed the antagonism between Aws and K͟hazraj into true brotherhood and spiritual love, even though blood had been spilled between them, and hostility and hatred had taken firm root?* But had He done so, test and purification would have been voided, and the good could not have been distinguished from the wicked, the benefits of trial and tribulation would have been lost, and the realities of all things would have remained concealed. In sum, should an insightful person meditate upon God's consolation and solace, His admonitions of patience, His reminders of what happened to past nations and bygone peoples, and, finally, His reproof and censure of the desire to perform miracles which are reposited in these verses, this would provide sufficient knowledge of the circumstances relating to signs and the consequences of demanding miracles. This is obvious to the perspicacious and those who possess a knowledge of the Book.

Among these verses is His saying in the Surah of the Cow, "And those who know not say, 'Why does God not speak to us? Why does a sign not come to us?' So spoke those before them similar words; their hearts are much alike. Yet We have made clear the signs unto a people who are certain."[23] That is, those who do not know the meaning of evidence and proof and are ignorant of the consequences of demanding miracles and the effects of seeking them said, "If Muḥammad is a messenger from God, why does God not speak to us, as He spoke to the children of Israel in the days of Moses, or cause a miracle to appear such as those performed by past prophets?"

*Aws and K͟hazraj were two feuding clans among the pre-Islamic Arabs.

God replied to them that this utterance resembles what the unbelievers of old used to say in refutation of the prophets and in rejection of their missions. The similarity of their statements gives evidence that their hearts are alike, for statements proceed from the heart. As Jesus said, trees are known by their fruits. If, for the past peoples, proposing miracles was a cause of their rejection and repudiation of prophets, and if it led them to perdition and ruination, then it will be so also for their successors, until the Primal Essence returns on the Day of Judgment—the Day when the people rise up before the Lord of the worlds. This is proved by the verse: "Even so We cause it to enter the hearts of the sinners—they believe not in it, though the wont of the ancients is already gone."[24]

Also among such verses is God's saying in the Surah of the House of 'Imran, "Those same men said, 'God has made a covenant with us, that we are not to believe in any Messenger until he brings to us a sacrifice devoured by fire.' Say: 'Messengers have come to you before me bearing clear signs, and with that of which you spoke; why therefore did you slay them if you speak truly?' "[25]

The traditions explain that the Jews met with the Prophet Muḥammad and said that God's wont in distinguishing the true from the false was that when a prophet claimed to be a messenger from God and his people opposed him, they should make two sacrifices to God. Fire would then descend from the sky and consume the sacrifice of the genuine prophet, serving as a sign for him and a proof against his adversaries. This is an allusion to the story of Cain and Abel (the sons of Adam), and to what happened between Elijah the Prophet and the pagan prophets during the reign of Ahab, King of Israel (as is mentioned in the eighteenth chapter of 1 Kings in the Old Testament). The Jews therefore demanded that the Prophet perform this miracle for them, so that they might witness it and believe in him. But God commanded Muḥammad to reply that prophets and messengers had come previously with such signs, including the very miracle they demanded, so for what reason did they slay them and reject them if they now spoke truly in pledging to believe in him [Muḥammad] after he performed this miracle for them?

But the Jews were bewildered by this answer. They were astonished that they should be addressed this way: for it was the Samaritans who had rejected Elijah the Prophet, not the Jews. Moreover, the Jews who demanded this miracle from the Prophet had not even existed in the time of Elijah, to be blamed for the offenses of others or castigated for their denial and rejection. Elijah lived more than fifteen hundred years before the Prophet Muḥammad, and it was unfair of the latter to direct this censure at the Jews of his own time. Insofar as they missed his purpose and were ignorant of his real meaning, they exposed their denial and rejection, uncovered the face of arrogance and censure, and demonstrated their unawareness of the nature of genesis and creation, and their heedlessness of the realities intended by the words "death," "life," "resurrection," and "return." In them God's saying was fulfilled: "Nay, they deny what their knowledge doth not encompass, though its interpretation has not yet come to them."[26]

Other relevant verses include God's saying in the Surah of the Story: "Yet when the truth came to them from Us, they said 'Why has he not been given the like of what Moses was given?' But they, did they not disbelieve also in what Moses was given aforetime? They said, 'A pair of sorceries mutually supporting each other.' They said, 'We disbelieve both.' Say: 'Bring a Book from God that gives better guidance than these, and follow it, if you speak truly.''' And God's saying in the Surah of Thunder: ''The unbelievers say: 'Why has a sign not been sent down upon him from his Lord?' Say: 'God leads astray whomsoever He will and He guides to Him all who are penitent.' Those who believe and whose hearts find rest in the mention of God—in the mention of God do hearts find rest.''[27] There are many such clear verses and explanations, which indicate that God refused to work miracles when they were proposed by the supercilious or when those who demanded a test raised their objections. Neither in the Gospel nor in the mighty Qur'án can the slightest reliance on ''proof-by-miracle'' be found, or the least suggestion of a compliance with any demand for signs. This is simply owing to their irrelevance, to the fact that resort to them would nullify the effect and benefit of God sending a prophet, and to the people's ignorance of the conditions for evidence and proof. It is apparent from our lengthy and detailed discourse above that the Prophet Muḥammad presented the Holy Book itself as evidence for the authenticity of his assertions because of the light, guidance, and mercy God had reposited therein. He refused to perform the miracles proposed to him because of the error, devastation, and calamity that would ensue.

It can be deduced from the above that the miracles related in the written biographies and the traditions of the Prophet can be depended on only if they do not contradict the clear text of the Qur'án, and that these should only be taken as supporting evidence and secondary proof. If these sources contain something at variance with the explicit verses of the Qur'án and the

Gospel, however, then they are utterly without foundation and may not be cited as evidence. Understanding this matter presents no difficulty or problem if hearts are not burdened with veils and fetters. The established rule accepted and used by the people of knowledge and wisdom is that those miracles are true and indubitable which derive from the universal and all-encompassing nature of the Holy Spirit. This has been established for us by the ancients and we have seen it in the moderns. Everything else is deception, delusion, fantasy, and daydream. It is like lightning without a storm, clouds without rain. This has become apparent to us from an understanding of the degree to which miracles constitute proof. We have thus devoted a prolonged discussion to this matter, applying rational evidence to the divine Book, and this should suffice the seekers of guidance and the possessors of knowledge.

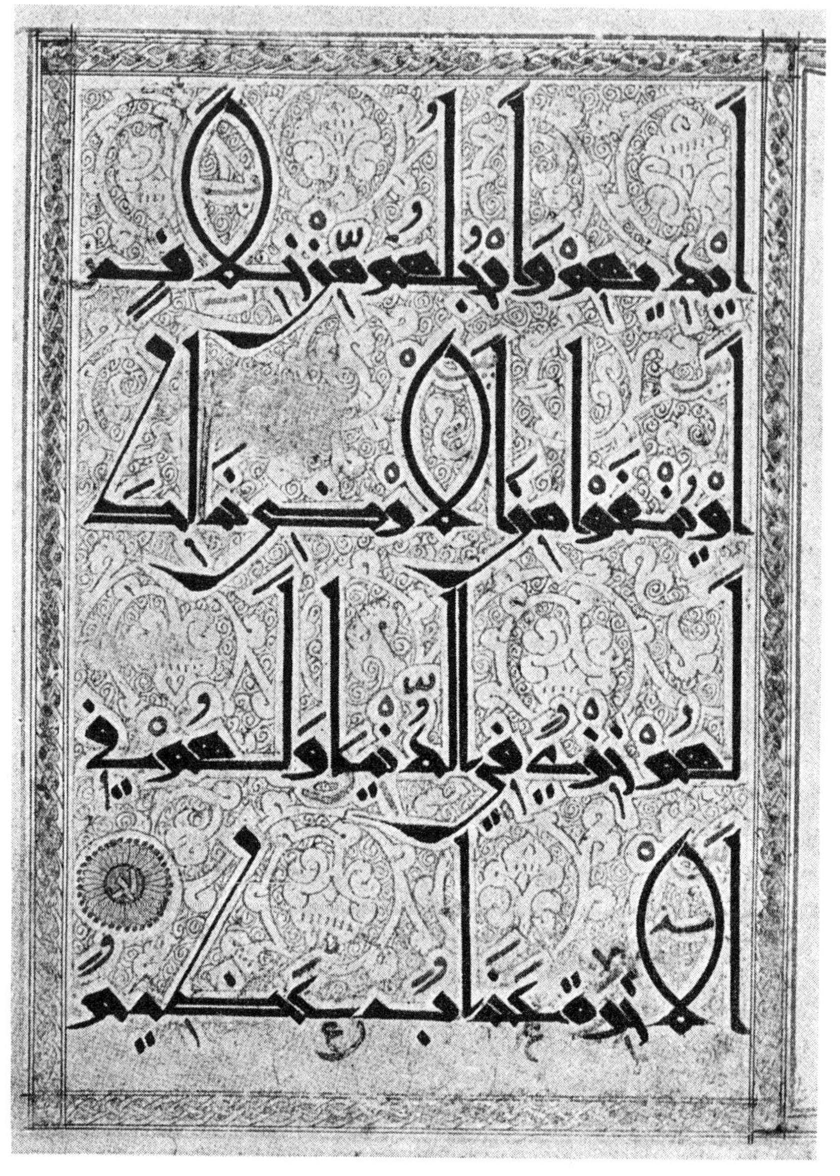

PAGE FROM THE QUR'ÁN
in Kufic script. Persian, eleventh century. Museum Dahlem, Berlin.

Why the Book Itself Is the Best Miracle

Let us now speak about the reason for which the Book itself constitutes a proof, and the inimitability of the celestial revelation. This is also a question that has been much discussed, on which opinions have differed, and which has ended in dispute among the learned. They have determined this matter to be ambiguous, and so have lost the truth because of their remoteness from the fount of life and their preference for bitter salt water over sweet pure water.

Know, O Sayyid from Sind—may God pour out for you the wine of purity and bring you near to the Dayspring of Light, the Dawning Theophany—that there is no argument or dispute between the nations concerning the conclusive authority of the Word of God or of divine revelation. Controversy and debate center solely on the distinguishing characteristics whereby the speech of the Creator may be known from the speech of the creatures, and whereby divine revelation may be distinguished from human invention.

Although we have mentioned this question above in a fashion that will suffice to inform the discerning, the summary and concise nature of our earlier discussion did not enable us generally to achieve its purpose. This is because hearts are encrusted with the rust of idle fancies, and are seduced by contrived dogmas and the vain flourishes of theology. First, we shall record the views of various communities on this issue. Then we shall follow this by presenting our own opinion. We shall leave judgment on this question to those of sound discrimination and undeviating thought, putting our trust in God, the Lord of the worlds, who is our highest aim and the highest aim of all in the heavens and on the earth.

As for the followers of the Gospel, they believe, as the eminent Austrian clergyman Pfander has demonstrated and established in his book *The Balance of Truth,* [28] and others have shown in other works, that any words that quench the need of the spirit for salvation are divine words and heavenly revelation. For it is undeniable that the spirit by its very nature stands in need of, and seeks to arrive at, a state of equanimity through true salvation, eternal life, and changeless bliss. Therefore, if words exist by which the spirit may attain serenity in reaching this desired state, this hoped-for goal, then no doubt will remain that they are the speech of God. This characteristic solely pertains, they assert, to the Holy Gospels and is lacking in the scriptures of other religions, for example, in the books of the Islamic, Buddhist, and Hindu communities, and so forth. This is, in short, their position concerning the recognition of the Word of God and the means of distinguishing between it and mortal speech.

However, any perspicacious scholar will realize that this characteristic is not an objective one which can silence opponents or undermine their proofs. Rather, this is simply an allegation that begs the question. For every religious community, and their scholars in particular, affirms and believes that divine benefits are confined solely to its own scriptures. Does not the Holy Qur'án assert and proclaim, "In the mention of God do hearts find rest."[29] Do not the "Buddhist" peoples of China believe in the book of Confucius, the founder of their religion and the legislator of their laws?* Do they not hold that it is the cause of salvation, the source of life, the first cause of serenity to all hearts, and the instiller of delight in the breasts of men? Do not the Hindus believe in the book of Bídpáí, and the Zoroastrians in the Zend Avesta—just as Christians believe in the Gospel and the Jews in the Torah?†

Indeed, quite often hearts have been, and are, attracted—have been, and are, brought to tranquility—by books other than the Holy Scriptures of the various religions. Sufi mystics are attracted by the works of their masters, and the Druze and extremist Shí'ís by the sayings of their great ones. What then, is the criterion that can decide between this plethora of claims and can distinguish the preferred books from among these divers writings? It has thus been demonstrated that the distinguishing characteristic affirmed by the aforementioned scholar is not an objective one, nor is it a clear criterion.

As for the learned in Islam, they discovered affirmations in the Qur'án that it is a divine proof and a heavenly sign, and that no one but God could produce

*Confucius (551–479 B.C.) was a Chinese teacher and scholar whose ideas of "heaven," "humanity," the "superior man," and the "doctrine of the mean" had a profound influence on Chinese culture. His basic teachings are contained in the *Analects*. He was not a religious teacher in the usual sense, but a philosopher whose ideas contained a spiritual component. 'Abdu'l-Bahá called him a moral renewer but did not categorize him as a prophet. (See *Some Answered Questions*, p. 165.) Shoghi Effendi termed him a moral reformer rather than a prophet. (See Shoghi Effendi, *Letters from the Guardian to Australia and New Zealand 1923–1957* [Sydney: National Spiritual Assembly of the Bahá'ís of Australia, Inc., 1970] p. 41.)

†Bídpáí is the Perso-Arabic name for Vidyapat, the Hindu sage to whom a book of wisdom stores was ascribed. In Arabic, this book was known as *Kalilah wa Dimnah*, from Arabic transliterations of the Sanskrit names of two animal characters.

The Zend Avesta is the Holy Book of the Zoroastrian religion.

words such as these, and that falsehood could not enter its presence or follow upon it. But they differed as to the reason for this inability and the cause of this inimitability. For it is self-evident that simply composing a book and stringing phrases together, even if the author be illiterate, cannot be counted a miracle or accepted as a proof. Some have asserted that the very sequence and style of the Qur'án verses constitute a miracle, and that no one could organize words in this special style or convey meanings in the form of words in this particular arrangement. Some have said that the Qur'án's inimitability derives from the fact that it contains prophecies of future events—such as its prophecy that the Byzantines would defeat the Persians in a few years (that is, within ten years from the revelation of the verse).* There are many similar prophecies that mortal minds could not have foreseen prior to their occurrence, nor could the people imagine them before they happened.

To see the falsehood of these two positions and the weakness of the proof they represent does not require great effort. Most learned men have not considered them any sort of proof. It is obvious that merely setting words and terms in order is not normally an impossible matter, whatever their style and arrangement. Likewise for the second view. For the verse must intrinsically constitute a proof, even before any prophecy related therein comes true. If faith depended on the fulfillment of what is prophesied in the verses, the people would be justified in continuing their unbelief and denial until such time as the prophecies are fulfilled. This is clearly a fallacy, and religions could not soundly proceed on this basis.

*Qur'án 30:1–5, revealed ca. 615–16 A.D., correctly predicted ultimate victory for the Byzantines in their war with the Persians.

No doubt there are in the Qur'án, and in the other Holy Books, many prophecies of future events the knowledge of which is of consequence to nations. These relate to their salvation or ruin. They include the striking of the Hour, which the Books of God have referred to with mighty names and divers designations, such as the Day of God, the Day of the Lord, the Resurrection Day, the Day of Sorrow, the Day of Encounter, and so on. These have been further clarified by the traditions of the Prophet as the Day on which the Mahdí will appear, and the Spirit of God [Jesus] will arise. The Qur'án mentions all the events associated with that magnificent Day, the advent of the Great Announcement, including its fullness, its particulars, its conditions and signs, and its appointed place and time. Those who know the Book well shall recognize this, and its intimates are aware of it. Certainly, knowing these prodigious events to which the world of being was destined to give birth and prophesying their specific dates in pellucid detail is a stupendous marvel and an imposing deed, which even a contentious ignoramous or an obdurate quibbler could not deny. Therefore, a reasoning man may consider such prophecy, from this point of view, a powerful miracle and a tremendous sign.

The Commander of the Faithful, 'Alí ibn Abí Ṭálib, whom God singled out in bestowing upon him His most excellent favors and mightiest gifts, alluded to this point in many of his eloquent talks and precious discourses. Among these is one quoted by 'Abd Rabbihi in his book *The Priceless Necklace* from al-Ḥárith al-A'war al-Hamadání. 'Alí is reported to have said, "I heard the Apostle of God say that the Book of God contains the mention of what came before you, an announcement of what shall come after you, and a judgment concerning what is among you. It is a decisive judgment, not a jest. The heart's inclinations do not stray from it, and the learned are never sated with it. It never wears out from overuse and its wonders never pall. Should a tyrant forsake it, God will break him, and whoso seeks guidance elsewhere, God will lead him astray. It is the mighty cord of God, the most great mention, the path of rectitude. Embrace it, O A'war."[30] What we have said has established that there are prophecies of future events in the Qur'án such as human reason could not have perceived before their occurrence. However, the ability to understand these abstruse allusions and to discern these truths in the depths of the Book's verses is not a common one, nor are these matters explicit and manifest so that anyone can behold them and comprehend them.

The proof must be complete for all and the sign must be perfect for everyone and, from this point of view, the Qur'án becomes a consummate proof and an irrefutable miracle. How can it be otherwise, when the Holy Scriptures themselves contain clear statements that the interruption of their verses—that is, their original, intended meanings—will only become evident on the Last Day? This refers to the resurrection of the Spirit [Jesus], the advent of the Manifestation of the Cause of God, and the dawning of the glory of the Divine Countenance from the earth's horizon upon the easts and wests. Before the arrival of that awesome and terrible Day, and the appearance of the Preexistent Lord, the original meanings intended in the prophecies are veiled and sealed with God's own seal. Without an understanding of them, the doors are barred and blocked by the power of God. For this reason, the commentaries on scripture by the learned have, from the revelation of the Torah until that of the Bayán,* been cold, barren, rigid, and insipid. Indeed, they are misleading, misguiding, distorted, and corrupt.

The Prophet Muḥammad referred to this truth in the famous saying wherein he states, "A time will come upon my community when nothing will remain of Islam among them save the name, or of the Qur'án save its script. They will call others to faith but will be the most remote of peoples from it. Their mosques will be filled to capacity, but desolate of any guidance. The jurisprudents of that time will be the most wicked beneath the sky; they will be the cause of the tribulations and these will rebound upon them." This noble tradition is explicit concerning the weakness of commentaries and their distance from the truth. For if the commentaries now existing in such great numbers were at all sound, it would not be possible for his words "or of the Qur'án save its script" to be fulfilled.

In this regard, I have been struck by one of the discourses of 'Alí ibn Abí Ṭálib, the Commander of the Faithful, which is included in *The Path of Eloquence.* We shall quote it here for the pure of heart and the illumined in vision. In spite of its brevity, it attains, in its superior oratory and relevance to the prophetic traditions, the Qur'án, and the state of the Islamic community today, a pinnacle beyond which there is no higher point of ascent for the onlooker, no loftier summit for the mind, save the Word of God and that of His Apostle. He said, in the midst of his discourse:

> Verily, a time will come upon you wherein nothing will be more concealed than the truth,

*The book of laws revealed in 1848 by the Báb (1819–1850).

nothing more manifest than falsehood, and nothing more numerous than lies about God and His Apostle. The people of that time will possess no commodity more difficult to sell than the Book when it is correctly recited, or one more in demand when its passages are misinterpreted. There will be throughout all lands nothing more detested than good deeds, or more renowned than evil ones. The reciters of the Qur'án will have cast it away, and those who memorize it will have deliberately erased it from their minds. The Book and its disciples will, on that day, be ostracized and outcast, two friends together on the road, to whom no one will offer shelter. The Book and its disciples will be, in that age, among the people and yet neither among them nor with them. For error is incompatible with guidance.

Even though the Book and its disciples might come together, the people would agree to keep separate. They would disperse from the community—as if they were the leaders of the Qur'án rather than it being their leader. Nothing will remain of it among them save the name; they will know nothing of it save its calligraphy and script. Before, they had not made an example of the righteous by maiming them, or called their sincerity towards God a lie, or punished good deeds with the penalties for crimes. They who preceded you perished because they went on hoping for too long and their allotted terms expired. Then the Promised One descended, by whom excuses are rejected and upon whom repentance has no effect, and with whom are the calamity and the affliction.[31]

The words "Promised One" in this noble address refer to the One whom God promised every religious community He would make manifest at the end of their dispensations, such as the Mahdí among the Muslims, the Messiah among the Jews, and the resurrection of the Spirit for all nations. Thus will the appointed time come to pass. The days will reach their end on a Day when the Lord will descend in the shadow of the clouds. This is not, as some commentators have interpreted it, a reference to death, since no one's death can cause the devastation of nations. Nor does it refer to a particular nation rather than others, nor one individual as opposed to others, because the door of repentance will not be closed upon an entire nation because of the daily deaths of its citizens. Rather, the door of repentance is barred to a community when its Promised One appears and its limited course of life comes to an end. As the famous tradition puts it: "The door of repentance shall not be barred until the sun rises from the west."

In sum, were an astute person to meditate and reflect on what every messenger has prophesied in his book concerning his community's future conditions—how it will pass through stages, rise and fall, and finally meet its end—he would recognize how remote the existing commentaries are from the true intentions of the Book. The traditions and sayings of the Prophet Muḥammad have made this clear, with their references to the future condition of the Islamic community. And these have been further elucidated and reiterated in 'Alí's discourse. No doubt remains for anyone without a desire to delude himself that these commentaries (in spite of their great length, their prolixity, and their diverse and varied styles of rhetoric) remain remote from the original intention of the verses, have strayed from the truth reposited in the divine Scriptures, and have kept the people far from the ultimate and greatest bestowal, the most glorious, weighty, and mighty gift. This the prophets clearly proclaimed in prophetic glad tidings: all the ancient Holy Scriptures comprise it and preserve it.

To demonstrate the extreme obscurity of these meanings—that is, of the prophecies related to future events—it will suffice to point out that, in spite of the fact that these books contain all the particulars and generalities of the prophecies and their appointed times, the nations rejected them and the people of the world ignored them, save only those whom God singled out for the light of awareness and whom He awakened with the spirit of discernment. These are few in number and, indeed, as the Imám 'Alí said, are forsaken and ostracized. As for the majority, they are ignorant of these meanings. They have even supposed that the Resurrection Day is other than the Day the Spirit of God [Jesus] will arise, and that the Hour refers to something other than the Hour of the advent of the Manifestation of God's Cause. Their idle fancies and vain imaginations have invented absurd, impossible matters and astonishing, unreasonable events concerning the meaning of that mighty Day. The prudent scholar or anyone with a discerning intellect can only stand in utter amazement and bewilderment before their interpretations of the meanings of "the Path," "the Balance," "the Accounting," "the Book," "the Gathering Together," and "the Resurrection."

It suffices to demonstrate their remoteness from, and their ignorance of, the Book's realities that ibn-Khaldun, the North African thinker, expressed doubts in regard to the soundness of the traditions that spoke of the appearance of the promised Mahdí.[32] His position was that the Qur'án is devoid of any such prophecies, and that no verse had been revealed on this matter. This betrays his ignorance of the meaning of "the Resurrection," the reality of "the Return," the intended significance of "the Hour," the concept of "the Calamity," the purport of "the Quaking," and the like. All these sublime concepts are truths that the traditions of the Prophet have explained by referring to the appearance of the Mahdí, the arising of the Spirit of God, the renewal of the world, the expiration of the terms allotted to the nations, the dawning of the light of the generous Lord upon earth, and the muteness of all voices before the rise of His great call.

It is amazing, even laughable (but at the same time a cause for weeping), that those who came after ibn-Khaldun, though they accepted the authority of Muslim consensus, followed his minority opinion on this matter, although on practically no other question was there as much consensus in the Islamic community as on this one. If you leaf through all the books composed before ibh-Khaldun, you will see that past scholars—God rest their souls in peace—were unanimous, in spite of their differences in legal rites and intellectual schools, in their agreement and consensus that the Mahdí would truly appear, that this was something foreordained and irrevocably decreed. They even termed his appearance "the first Resurrection" and "the lesser Hour."

In the period of seven centuries and more from the passing of the Prophet Muḥammad until the birth of ibn-Khaldun, not one of the learned can be found who dared to deny the Mahdí's appearance or presumed to declare all the prophecies concerning him to be weak in their authenticity. These later scholars thus set themselves in opposition to the public and tampered with this renowned consensus. They destroyed the most cherished hopes of the reformers, severed the cord of prosperity to which the community had held fast, and barred the gates of victory in their faces. For this reason, you find most Sunní doctors of law in an astonishing state of despair over the future of the community and its ability to ascend to heights of glory and exaltation. They are firmly convinced of its retrogression, its decline, and its failure. This is referred to in the tradition that the Mahdí will arise only at a time of despair and despondency.

Even more startling than all this is that, though they doubt the appearance of the Mahdí and account the prophecies concerning him weak in their authenticity, they are nevertheless entirely certain that Jesus will descend from heaven and have accounted the traditions concerning his descent as sound. If one asks them about the source of such prophecies in the Qur'án,* which claims to hold within it the explanation of every thing in detail, they are unable to answer. They are perplexed in their discourse and remain ignorant of the realities they were promised in the Book.

*If the learned of our time are asked about the prophecy in the Qur'án that Jesus will return, they cite the verse, "There is not one of the People of the Book but will assuredly believe in him before his death." (4:159). However, this verse does not allude to the advent of Jesus, but to the faith the People of the Book had in him before his death. The point is to find a prophecy of his coming. It is possible that the referent of the possessive pronoun "his" in "his death" is the People of the Book. That is, that because of the clarity of his proof and the manifest truth of his religion, no one among the People of the Book will fail to believe in Jesus. There is no evidence that the referent of the possessive pronoun in "his death" is Jesus himself.—ABU'L-FAḌL.

[Cf. Geoffrey Parrinder, *Jesus in the Qur'án* (London: Faber and Faber, 1965), p. 108.]

They know nothing of the verses of the Qur'án but the script; they taste nothing of the fruits of paradise save the rinds. Imám 'Alí's prediction is fulfilled in them, and the Prophet's announcement is realized in them.

If the intent of what we have just written (which has carried us into an uncharted, rugged, and difficult subject) is understood, then it has been established that, as we mentioned above, the gift of understanding the realities of the prophecies in the Holy Book concerning the future is not a common one. Not everyone can understand these prophecies, nor can this proof be valid for everyone. Rather, this is a special endowment for which God has singled out His chosen ones and with which He has inspired His friends and lovers. This being the case, it would be inaccurate to term the Qur'án a universal proof or a sufficient miracle in this regard.

Many of the learned, particularly in the Middle Ages, held that the cause of the Qur'án's inimitability lay in the eloquence of its verses and the rhetorical excellence of its phrases, such as all the nations were incapable of matching, and with which the peoples of the earth were incapable of competing. This view arose because Arabic language sciences spread and became popular among the scholars of the second, third, and fourth Islamic centuries. These scholars made great advances in the literary arts and ascended to the highest ranks under the 'Abbásid, Fáṭimid, and [Spanish] Umayyad caliphates. The arts of writing and oratory flourished among them; the tree of eloquence and rhetoric grew lofty and gave fruit.

Most of them, if not all of them, however, remained engrossed in their carnal appetites and drowned in their decadent pleasures. Their compositions explicitly bear witness to this: their biographies openly speak of it. And such misdeeds are certain to blind the vision of the heart, remove one far from the path of rectitude, and lead one away from the road of guidance and maturity. So these scholars discovered that the eloquence of the Qur'án's verses is of the highest order, that its words are well arranged to a sublime degree. And they found that they themselves were unable to equal it and that their pens were powerless to imitate it. Therefore, they came to believe that the eloquence and rhetorical excellence of the verses accounted for their inimitability and produced their supreme distinction.

This belief spread throughout the community, and most of its eminent men accepted it. The religious scholars gave it currency in their views, recording it in their books. For this was the belief of the secretaries and ministers, and it was the opinion of the high officials in the secretarial department of the state, who held the reigns of authority in the far-flung caliphate. It is said that the people follow the religion of their rulers, since they emulate their kings in their views and behavior.

The essential piece of evidence supporting this view is that the Prophet Muḥammad presented the Qur'án as a challenge. He stated in various places in the Book that the Arabs should, if they refused to accept that the Qur'án was from God, attempt to produce its like. He affirmed and predicted that they would never be able to produce the like of it—even if everyone on earth were to agree and to aid in the attempt. Likewise, he proclaimed that falsehood could not approach it from in front or from behind.[33] That is, no mendacious claimant, no false prophet or lying impostor would be able, without God's permission, to put together a book like the Qur'án and attribute it to

God. Nor would they ever succeed in giving it such currency in the world that it would become established or spread among the nations.

The rulers and chiefs, the poets and orators of the Arabs—a people notorious for inflexibility and coarseness—failed to produce anything like the Qur'án, and they were silenced by this proof. This was so in spite of their fierce resistance to the Prophet. They expended every conceivable effort and braved hardships and horrors in endeavoring to efface his Cause and obstruct his religion, in attempting to overcome his followers and war against his supporters. Certainly, if they had been able, they would have produced something like it, and would have avoided any need to endure these hardships and expend their blood and wealth in resisting his religion.

It may be concluded from all this that the Arabs were utterly incapable of producing anything like the Qur'án, and that they were helpless before this proof. And if the orators and rhetoricians of the Arabs, in spite of their renown for having mellifluous tongues and eloquent speech, thus failed, this necessarily and self-evidently establishes that all other peoples of the world would have found themselves similarly impotent. For it is absurd to expect that a non-Arab who is altogether ignorant of the Arabic language could produce an Arabic book which the most accomplished rhetoricians of the Quraysh tribe and the champions of Arabic letters could not match. All this demonstrates the impotence of all the earth's nations and the helplessness of Arabs and non-Arabs alike. This is the meaning of the brilliant miracle and the heavenly and splendorous sign.

This represents a summary of the proofs and arguments that establish the inimitability of the Qur'án in regard to its eloquence and rhetorical excellence. The outward beauty of the Holy Book enchanted past scholars, but they remained heedless of its implications for the next world. They filled tomes and volumes with such verses and devoted treatises and books to them. Al-Báqillání's book on the inimitability of the Qur'án should suffice as an example.[34] For it is the most prolix and elaborate of such works—and, he claimed, the most charming and admirable. He adorned it with the precious speeches of the House of Abú Sufyán and rounded it out with the most splendid discourses of Banú Marwán, as if the oratory of Ziyád and Ḥajjáj add to the power of his evidence or help perfect his proof.

However, anyone acquainted with research and investigation, who possesses some insight concerning theories, and has sound discrimination in the rational sciences, will discern the weakness of their proof and the feebleness of their evidence. This is so in various respects. We shall mention just a few of them here, that perhaps God by His grace will protect the people of our time from the errors of the ancients and guard them from the blunders of those that followed them, so that they will not stumble as have their predecessors.

First, if the Qur'án's inimitability lay in its eloquence and rhetorical excellence, it could not constitute a universal proof and there would be no difference between it and all other miracles. For eloquence and rhetorical excellence are characteristics that only specialists can perceive. Such specialists are obviously extremely few in number in relation to the nonspecialists. Moreover, the world's great peoples, such as the ordinary Arabs, the Iranians, the Turks, the Indians, the Chinese, the Europeans, the Americans, and the Africans, know no Arabic and therefore cannot recognize the inimitability of the Qur'án. They could only admit that this constitutes a proof by accepting the verdict of the small number of people who are learned in Arabic rhetoric. This, in turn, is nothing less than blind imitation—the acceptance of someone else's statement without independent evidence—just as every people has accepted the statements of a tiny number of persons concerning the appearance of miracles from the prophets and messengers, and even from Sufi masters and ascetics. There is thus no difference between it and other miracles and supernatural events that the people relate of their great men and leaders. This will doubtless lead to a contradiction between the various proofs, a conflict of evidence, and will result in narrow conclusions, as will be obvious to those who judge with insight and justice.

All this assumes that experts in Arabic rhetoric will concur that they are unable to produce the like of the Qur'án, that it transcends mortal skill in its excellent arrangement and its perfection. Should they fail to concur in this, the Qur'án would not even attain the same status as other miracles, much less that of a universal proof and an irrefutable miracle. The scholars and people of knowledge know very well that the Arab rhetoricians, from the appearance of the Prophet until our own day, have never agreed on this matter in any century. No century passed but some scholar denied that the Qur'án reached the level of inimitability in the eloquence of its speech and the excellent style of its utterance. We shall here mention a few of their criticisms and a summary of their statements.

No reasonable man doubts that such great Christian authors and writers as Buṭrus al-Bustání, compiler of *The Sea of Seas,*[35] the renowned scholar Náṣíf al-Yázijí, author of *The Meeting of Two Seas,*[36] and his son Ibráhím (as well as other great rhetoricians and specialists in language, the names and works of which the brief compass of this essay must exclude from mention) do not look upon the noble Qur'án in the same way as the Muslim community does. They do not recognize that it is inimitable in its eloquence and rhetorical excellence, as Muslims do.

The rational cause for the disagreement on this question is that the attribute of goodness in all perceptible things such as goodness of speech, goodness of voice, goodness of luck, goodness of character, and so on, is a subjective matter that has no specific boundary, limited range, or any known quantity. Reason, therefore, cannot judge definitely that such and such level of eloquence constitutes the dividing line beyond which the utmost human skill cannot reach. From this premise we must conclude that even a specialist in rhetoric cannot specify this level or make a decision about it, how much less one who is untrained.

Thus you see that the most eloquent of the Arabs and the leaders of the Quraysh tribe, such as Naḍr ibn al-Ḥárith, 'Utbah ibn Rabí'ah, Abú Sufyán ibn Ḥarb, Shaybah ibn Rabí'ah, and Ka'b ibn al-Ashraf used to ridicule the Holy Qur'án and deem producing the like of it a trifle. They proclaimed and asserted in full public view: "If we wished, we could speak like that. These are only the fables of the ancients." While the illiterates among the Muslims, such as Salmán the Persian, Bilál the Ethiopian, Miqdád, and Abú Dharr—who were not particularly eminent, nor were they reckoned knights in the arena of rhetoric—recognized that the Qur'án was the Word of God which had descended from heaven, and that it constituted sufficient proof to all who dwell in the worlds of creation. This is because the ability to taste the sweetness of the Remembrance* and delight in this discourse depends on purity and sincerity of heart, not on the knowledge of the arts of rhetoric and recitation.

Second, if the irrefutability of the Qur'án rested upon its eloquence and rhetoric, then believing in it would require knowledge of this art. It would be incumbent on whoever wished to have faith in it to learn the science of the Arabic language, including lexicography, syntax, inflection, rhetoric, exposition, the use of metaphors, and so on. For accepting something without knowledge of it is accepting an unknown; and this is necessarily a foolish error. To require that every seeker of guidance study these branches of learning would clearly cause impediments and obstacles, and this is invalid according to reason.

To clarify this question, let us give an unambiguous example. Let us suppose you were to call the Christians or the Hindus to the religion of the Prophet Muḥammad, as it is commanded in God's words, "Call thou to the way of thy Lord with wisdom and good admonition," and His words, "Let there be one nation of you, calling to good."[37] Now, it is obvious that the one being taught will seek from you a proof for the soundness of Islam's foundation and the truthfulness of its Prophet. Should you cite as evidence the miracles handed down in the traditions, he would refute you by quoting the explicit verses of the Qur'án, as has been seen to happen quite often. Nor will it be of any use at that point to attempt to contradict his assertion by appealing to the Holy Gospel, insofar as it also contains a rejection of miracles, since our lord Jesus refused to

*A title of the Qur'án.

comply with the Jews when they demanded signs. For the fact that blind imitation of one's forefathers is practiced by those who inherit their religion does not justify it in the religion of individual effort.

Finally, this debate must certainly end in your citing the glorious Qur'án, the noble Book, as evidence. At that point, he will reply to you that authoring a book, even though the author be illiterate, hardly proves that one is a prophet. He will ask what the distinguishing characteristic of the Qur'án is, that he may be sure that it was revealed by the Lord, the All-Merciful. You will reply that the Holy Qur'án reached such levels of eloquence and rhetorical excellence that no human being could produce a comparable chapter—even a small one—though they all gather together and aid each other. Nor could they give life to the dead, transform a staff into a writhing serpent, ascend into heaven, or perform other marvelous signs.

Let us suppose the man then answers, "You have explained the matter superbly and have presented a perfect proof! Now, you will excuse me for a moment while I go study rhetoric and exposition, that I might acquire some discernment in the matter of religion and avoid being ignorant." Then your proof will necessarily fail, and it will be useless to continue to argue on the basis of this fallacy. For he is correct in his statement and his answer has hit the mark. Assume that he learns Arabic over a period of ten years or more, and progresses and excels in the literary arts so that he becomes an eloquent and loquacious orator. Who will guarantee that after all this time he will recognize, along with the Muslim scholars, that the Qur'án attains the station of inimitability in its eloquence and rhetoric?

Who can say that he will not believe, along with the chiefs of the Quraysh tribe at the beginning of Islam, and the Christian scholars of our own day, that it is simply a compendium of ancient fables with no particular distinction over other classic books and compositions?

Third, the Holy Qur'án contains no mention, not even the slightest hint, that it is a proof or a miracle in regard to its eloquence and rhetoric. The fact is that in this manifest Book God widened the scope of evidence and the range of argument for the truth of the Qur'án and of His Prophet's mission. He employed all sorts of proofs which are known to scholars and are dear to the hearts of the pure ones whose souls are healthy and whose breasts are tranquil. These are ignored by the obtuse and denied by the ignorant, who have satisfied themselves with only the name of Islam, and only the calligraphy of the Qur'án.

As we have previously mentioned, the Qur'án itself states that it contains the explanation of all things. God said, "We have neglected nothing in the Book," and, in the Surah of Joseph, "It is not a tale forged, but a confirmation of what is before it, and a detailed exposition of all things, and a guidance, and a mercy to a people who believe."[38] These verses explicitly state that God did not neglect anything concerning religion or the Prophet's law, be it principles, auxiliaries, proofs, origins, or final events. He explained everything in detail; He plainly announced it in this glorious Scripture, the august and lauded Book. Thus was it said that "the heart's inclinations do not stray from it and the learned are never sated with it"; and "whoso seeks guidance elsewhere, God will lead him astray." Such promises and threats, such encouragement and warning, could be justly made only after God's bounty was completed, His proof perfected, His sign manifested, and His path made clear.

Is it reasonable to suppose, after all this, that God—who gave detailed expositions on everything in His Book—would neglect the question of the way this Book is proven, or would fail to clarify the cause of its inimitability? Would He have been ambiguous or misleading in explaining why it is indisputable? Did He stand in need of religious scholars and litterateurs to provide the details and to complete the argument for His Book, citing in its favor the discourses of Banú Marwán and embellishing it with the virtues of the House of Abú Sufyán? To God belongs the credit for the insight of the man who said:

> Matters at which the foolish laugh
> and at whose consequences the prudent weep.

These are some of the weaknesses in the argument from eloquence and some of the problems of employing rhetorical excellence as evidence. We have presented them as a reminder to the discerning, in order to broaden our thinking concerning the reality of the scriptures. It was not our intent to argue that the Holy Qur'án, that ancient Book,[39] did not attain the highest degree of eloquence and rhetorical excellence, or that anyone but God could produce its like in elegance and grace. God forbid! The people of Bahá, who cleave to the lofty and blessed Word, believe that all the descriptions, traits, virtues, and stations belonging to the Manifestations of the Cause of God are a miracle for the people, serving to confound their enemies. They are sanctified above likeness or similarity and are exalted above peer or equal. No one resembles them in any of their qualities. No soul can imitate any of their deeds.

It follows from what we have said that—just as the Prophet Muḥammad surpassed all other people in his generosity, munificence, beauty, splendor, patience, courage, knowledge, wisdom, forebearance, and compassion—so also he surpassed them in the eloquence of his tongue and the splendor of his utterance. For this reason, there are many passages wherein it was revealed that all human beings, no matter where they turn, stand powerless to produce a single verse like the verses of the Qur'án.

However, eloquence and rhetorical excellence are not obvious matters that any person can easily perceive and recognize. Only in this case would the proof become universal, the evidence made clear and the pathway opened to all classes of humanity, justice be done to every individual, and all pretexts and excuses be discredited. Rather, eloquence is a subtle, elusive quality that logicians would categorize as ambiguous. It has infinite levels and contains concealed subtleties, even for superb orators and authors. Therefore, we have maintained that even scholars of this art and brilliant rhetoricians cannot establish a fixed dividing line that can distinguish between the speech of the people and the Speech of God in regard to rhetoric and eloquence. This should suffice the people of insight.

As for the people of Bahá, the inmates of the Crimson Ark, who have cast away the burden of blind imitation and have raised the standard of independent investigation, they believe that the Word of

God surpasses other speech by virtue of its influence and success in guiding people, creating an independent religious community, and establishing a new law. Bahá'ís refer to these distinguishing characteristics as "creativeness" and "conquering power," and consider these sufficient for the recognition of holy verses and divine revelation.

A summary of the evidence for this argument is as follows. Let us suppose that someone challenges the people, using words that he attributes to God. Let us say he manifests perfect skill in guiding souls who are eager and seeking, vanquishes the nations that deny and hinder him, founds a thriving independent community, and establishes a new and abiding religious law. No doubt would then remain that his word is the Word of God which has descended from the heavens, and its refulgent power is the same power that has from time immemorial appeared from the messengers and prophets. The glorious Qur'án alludes to this point, saying, "God was desiring to verify the truth by His words and to cut off the unbelievers to the last remnant"; and further, "Those who argue concerning God after that answer has been made to Him, their argument is null and void in the sight of their Lord; anger shall rest upon them, and there awaits them a terrible chastisement."[40] This attribute is found only in the Books of God, and every person can perceive and understand it in them, whether he be learned or illiterate, Arab or non-Arab, Easterner or Westerner.

Who can doubt that it was the Torah alone which delivered the children of Israel from the gloom of ignorance into the light of faith, from the debasement of slavery into the glory of independence? Who can be unaware that it was the Gospel which allowed the peoples of Europe to ascend to monotheism from their pagan cults and to worship one God after adoring idols? Who does not know that the guidance of the Qur'án delivered the great nations dwelling between the Far East and the farthest limits of Africa from the noose of idolatry and fire worship into belief in and worship of one God? It was the light of this glorious Book alone that freed them from the shackles of corrupt doctrines and vile practices and gave them virtuous characters and sound beliefs.

It is true that one unacquainted with the facts may object that the Islamic religion attained its influence and became victorious by means of the swords of Arab warlords, rather than by divine utterance and spiritual triumph. Moreover, the Jews, Buddhists, and Hindus apply precisely the same criticism to Christianity that the Christians apply to Islam. They say that the Christian faith spread with the aid of Roman emperors and European despots, that it was established by the sword and by fire, and that as it spread rivers of blood flowed, as the histories of the Church bear witness and proclaim in every region.

This criticism, as the people of truth know, is a delusion that the discerning may simply dismiss. None but the foolish will cling to this feeble cord. For Islam was promulgated and spread among the Arabs before the Hijrah,* and Christianity expanded and grew before the triumph of Constantine. By the Life of God! Had these swords not been drawn for the sake of exalting the light of truth and of promulgating the word of faith—had it not been for the Gospel and the Qur'án—then these very same

*That is, before Muḥammad's emigration in 622 A.D. from Mecca, where he had no military force, to Medina, where the dispossessed Muslims took up arms.

swords would have been unsheathed in order to render paganism and idol worship victorious.

These huge armies, these powerful states, were also brought into being, formed, and set in motion by the influence of the Word, will, and permission of God. Without this, no society named "Christian" or "Islamic" ever would have existed, nor would any nation possess that power beyond which there is no other in the world of humanity. God has decreed, in His foreknowledge and perfect wisdom, the dispatch of messengers and prophets who are simple, illiterate, poor, indigent, and outcast. They are persecuted by kings and rulers, by the rich and haughty, and even by their own relatives. These messengers are purified above everything that might give them any advantage, including acquired knowledge, wealth and fortune, and the strength and glory that derive from the solidarity of one's people. This was so that every fair-minded person, even the philosophers who attribute everything to natural causes, must recognize that the force, the manifest power, which is apparent in the influence of their speech, in the victory of their religion, the exaltation of their Word, and the endurance of their law, is not attributable to any of these causes. Indeed, it was their enemies and resisters who enjoyed all these advantages. Rather, this force and power derive from the divine Will and depend on the unseen, celestial potency.

It was to this that the Qur'án referred when it said, "God is He Who raised up the heavens without pillars you can see."[41] In the holy *Book of Certitude*, the meaning of the term "heavens" was explained as referring to the religions.[42] Therefore, it is clear that God raised up the heavens of religion by His pristine will and His pure volition, not by the pillars of wealth or riches, dominion or sovereignty, glory or strength, knowledge or philosophy. These are things that the people recognize as pillars in the establishment of high temporal office and notable earthly rank. The word "heavens" was metaphorically applied to religion because of its loftiness and majesty. The term "pillar" was used in reference to the material causes we have mentioned because all of the supreme, elevated stations of the world of human dominion—including authority, leadership, sovereignty, glory, and so forth—are built and founded on these causes, and depend on them. This is a metaphor that is supremely graceful and fitting, and an expression that is both beautiful and eloquent. It is not possible to interpret the term "heavens" in this noble verse literally, to mean the sky. Anyone with any knowledge of astronomy knows that the physical sky cannot have pillars, since it is inconceivable that this outward sky should rest on any support, whether one depends on the ancient Ptolemaic form of astronomy or on the new European form.

In sum, Bahá'ís believe that these characteristics (that is, guiding souls, founding a new religion through overcoming the ancient faiths and transforming old customs) are the obvious distinguishing features that separate divine words from human compositions. They refer to these, as we have mentioned, as creativeness and conquering power. If the first soul who submits to the truth of any messenger's mission and accepts his law did not recognize this guidance within himself, and did not feel this triumph in his essence, then he would not be the first to believe, to respond, to follow and obey. For in all men the love of the religion of one's fathers is deeply entrenched, and the fear of changing its tenets and customs is firmly established in the depths of all hearts.

Guidance is the sign that most clearly distinguishes the truth of a prophet or messenger, since it is an attribute of the action involved and is related to the prophet's claim—as healing is to medicine, as knowledge of planes is to geometry, as buying and selling is to commerce, and as making doors and bedsteads is to carpentry. It is by virtue of the great and noble attribute of guidance that prophets are said to prophesy, messengers to deliver God's message, and divine legislators to give laws. Verily, He is the Creator, the All-Knowing! If you page through the glorious Qur'án, you will find that God cites this as His evidence on numerous occasions. He extolls the Qur'án as a proof by virtue of the guidance and mercy reposited therein. But one cannot find a single passage wherein He characterizes the Qur'án as the most eloquent of books or the most rhetorically distinguished of scriptures.

Consider the Surah of Stories where God says, "Yet when the truth came to them from Us, they said, 'Why has he not been given the like of what Moses was given?' But they, did they not disbelieve also in what Moses was given aforetime? They said, 'A pair of sorceries mutually supporting each other.' They said, 'We disbelieve both.' Say: 'Bring a Book from God that gives better guidance than these, and follow it, if you speak truly.'"[43] Notice that God silenced them with His words: "Then bring a Book from God that gives better guidance than these." He did not say, "Then bring a Book from God that is more eloquent than these or excels them in its rhetoric."

Likewise, in the Surah of the Spider, when they criticized the Prophet for not performing a miracle, God said, "They say, 'Why have signs not been sent down upon him from his Lord?' Say: 'The signs are only with God, and I am only a plain warner.' What, is it not sufficient to them that We have sent down upon thee the Book that is recited to them? Surely in that is a mercy, and a reminder to a people who believe."[44] God explained that the Qur'án's distinctive virtue over other miracles and its fitness above the others lies in its being a reminder and a mercy. He did not say, "Surely in that is eloquence and rhetorical excellence." In the beginning of the Surah of the Cow, God said, "*Alif. Lám. Mím.* That is the Book, wherein is no doubt, a guidance to the God-fearing."[45] He did not say, ". . . wherein is eloquence and rhetoric the like of which the entire world is incapable of producing." There are many such examples, as is not concealed from anyone who has been given a knowledge of the Holy Book and who knows the meaning of proof and decisive judgment.

Were eloquence and rhetoric the clear token, the apparent and distinctive sign, would not God have informed us of this, even if only in one verse? Would He not have warned us of this and clearly stated it, even if only in one passage of the Holy Book? For therein He left out nothing great or small, taking account of everything; and He neglected no proof or sign, mentioning and clarifying them all. Did He then forsake this one and leave it to al-Bágillání to complete it and achieve His purpose?

The people only fell into this error, produced this rubbish, stumbled so scandalously, and erred so grievously, because they forsook the shade of the boughs of the blessed prophetic Tree. They abandoned its delicate, newly harvested fruit, and cleaved instead to the branches of that tree described in the Qur'án.* And so they reaped only a harvest of regret and gathered only the brambles of folly. They continued in their transgression, persisted in their falsehood, wandered astray in their error, loitered in their ignorance, allowed torpor to overtake them, and engrossed themselves in their offenses. Their hearts hardened and their era was prolonged. Finally, the results of their heedlessness and folly and their hatred of the truth appeared, as the guides and leaders of the community had warned. The tragic outcome of all this is apparent to the wise and discerning, while the blind and the lost cannot see it, even though its outward signs loom clearly. These consequences include the disillusionment of the Muslim community, widespread anxiety, earthquakes and frightful calamities, continuing discord of a violent and dismal nature, estrangement among hearts, languor among the friends of God, the rallying of enemies, and the attacks of foes. These were generated by old hatreds kindled by feuds hidden within the breasts of ancient nations, and the stagnation caused by their dissensions was preferred by sick hearts. But most people are distracted and heedless of the consequences of their actions. They have opposed the Ark of Salvation which they were promised. Leave them, then, to cavort and to discuss this matter. The Morn they were promised has dawned.

It is known to the people of erudition that in the

*The tree described in the Qur'án is the evil tree of Zaqqúm, which is a symbol of the torture of hell. See Qur'án 44:43–46.

BAHÁ'Í INTERNATIONAL GROUP

Cairo, Egypt (April, 1907). Seated on Right: Ḥájí Niaz, Thornton Chase, and Mírzá Abu'l-Faḍl.

MÍRZÁ ABU'L-FAḌL (seated on chair)
with (l. to r.) Ali-Kuli Khan, Aḥmad Sohrab, and Ahamid Saraf

beginning, when the noble verse, "Then bring a surah like unto it," was revealed, the chiefs of the Quraysh tribe imagined that the Prophet Muḥammad was presenting the eloquence and rhetorical excellence of the Qur'án as a proof. They thus sought to resist him with the eloquence of their own words and to undermine his proof with the beauty of their own rhetorical discourses. They called him (God forbid!) an insane poet; and they thought the Word of God a ridiculous jest. They sarcastically said, and contemptuously proclaimed: "If we wished to produce the like of it, we could. These are naught but the fables of the ancients." The Prophet pointed out the way in which the Qur'án was its own proof and explained the reason for its conclusiveness. He silenced them by pointing to the guidance and compassion that God had reposited in the Qur'án, to the penetrating power of His Word, and to His ability to found a religious community.

They were thus dumbfounded, and their lamp was extinguished. At that point, they determined to resist the Prophet by force and violence, trading words for swords and proofs for war. They arose to attack him and rallied their forces to the struggle. The two sides prepared for battle and waged war. Finally, the forces of falsehood grew weak, the spirit of this band of wrongdoers was broken, the smoldering embers of idol worship were extinguished, and the cord from which the age of ignorance hung was severed. Debate and wrangling over the eloquence and rhetoric of the Qur'án ceased, until our scholars renewed the argument—employing this proof in their compositions, commenting on it in their testimonies, and arming themselves with it in their debates.

This is particularly true in recent times, when the mixing of populations has increased, tribes and nations have been united, the ties between all people have become more numerous, and the means of intercourse between all mankind have multiplied. Naturally, religious discussions between peoples have become more frequent, scholarly controversies have expanded, and sectarian disputes have become aggravated. Christian scholars have arisen to refute the proofs of the Muslims and to demonstrate the weakness of the evidence for establishing the truth of Islam based on the eloquence and rhetoric of the Qur'án, the inimitability and brilliance of its words. They have written essays and articles on this subject and have deceived hearts and minds with their assertions. Because, as we have explained, the virtues of rhetorical excellence and eloquence are unknown to the layman and are difficult to understand and obscure for most people, it is certain that their arguments will have an effect on many of the innocent, and their skepticism will create uncertainty in simple hearts.

Had our scholars followed, in their attempts to establish the Qur'án's miraculous quality, the path of the first believers and the rightly guided imams, they would have educated the community and filled this gap. Then all eyes would have been illumined and all hearts reassured. However, God, by virtue of His foreknowledge, His irrevocable decree, His hidden wisdom, and His secret tests, insisted on bringing to fruition all that whereof His messenger had warned them, and on punishing them for some of their previous misdeeds.

They have recorded among the sound traditions, from Abú Da'úd and at-Tirmidhí, from Thawbán, that the Prophet said: "If my community is put under the sword, they shall not escape it until the Resurrection Day. The Final Hour will not strike until some Muslim tribes match the pagans, and until some of them worship idols. There will arise among my community thirty liars, each of whom will claim that he is the Prophet of God. . . ." They have also transmitted, among the proofs of prophethood, a narrative from Abú Da'úd and al-Bayhaqí, from Thawbán: "The Prophet said, 'The nations will press in upon you as food in the bowl it rests in.' Someone asked, 'Because of the fewness of our numbers at that time?' The Prophet replied, 'No, on that day you will be many; but you will be like scum, like the debris of a flood. God will remove from the breasts of your enemies any fear of you and will cast feebleness in your hearts.' Someone asked, 'What feebleness?' The Prophet replied, 'Love of the world and aversion to death.'"

There are many such examples, in the authentic traditions, of prophecies made by the Prophet Muḥammad about the condition of the people of Islam. The succession of days and nights has proved him right; and the revolution of ages and epochs has brought these things to pass. Blessed is the soul that knows its origin and its end and is informed of its lewdness and its piety. Blessed are the hearts that have trembled at the wafting breezes of the Day of God. Blessed are the eyes that have been illumined by witnessing the signs of God, have kept watch for the flash of the lightning of guidance from the sanctuary of the divine presence, and have eagerly longed for the garden of eternity upon the field of martyrdom. These are the firm and the steadfast, upon whom rest the prayers of their Lord. They are those who gain.

THE ARCHANGEL MICHAEL
from a Cosmology by Qazvín. Baghdád, late fourteenth century. Courtesy of the Freer Gallery of Art, Smithsonian Institution, Washington, D.C.

A Refutation of Christian Criticisms of the Qur'án

We shall here quote some of what learned Christians have written in refutation of our scholars' argument based on the eloquence of the Qur'án. To these we shall add our own observations, so as to inform seekers and complete the proof sufficiently in this respect. We beseech God to confirm us with a spirit from Him. He is, verily, our Guardian in the beginning and the end.

The most amazing commentary we have seen in this regard is a work by the Englishman George Sale, which is entitled "Discourse on Islam." Háshim ash-Shámí, a Syrian Christian, translated it into Arabic and commented on it in detail. It was published by the American Religious Society in 1891 A.D. and distributed in Cairo, the capital of Egypt. In this brief essay we shall quote from the author, and from the translator and commentator, concerning the Qur'án's eloquence or lack thereof. For between their statements there exists the contradiction, conflict, disparity, and delusion that always characterize the views of those who reject God and oppose Him even though they have no ground to stand on. This is the text of the English scholar's remarks:

> Though it be written in prose, yet the sentences generally conclude in a long continued

rhyme, for the sake of which the sense is often interrupted, and unnecessary repetitions too frequently made, which appear still more ridiculous in a translation, where the ornament, such as it is, for whose sake they were made, cannot be perceived. However, the Arabians are so mightily delighted with this jingling, that they employ it in their most elaborate compositions, which they also embellish with frequent passages of, and allusions to, the Qur'án, so that it is next to impossible to understand them without being well versed in this book.

It is probable the harmony of expression which the Arabians find in the Qur'án might contribute not a little to make them relish the doctrine therein taught, and give an efficacy to arguments which, had they been nakedly proposed without this rhetorical dress, might not have so easily prevailed. Very extraordinary effects are related of the power of words well chosen and artfully placed, which are no less powerful either to ravish or amaze than music itself; wherefore as much has been ascribed to this part of rhetoric as to any other. He must have a very bad ear who is not uncommonly moved with the very cadence of a well-turned sentence; and Muḥammad seems not to have been ignorant of the enthusiastic operation of rhetoric on the minds of men, for which reason he has not only employed his utmost skill in these his pretended revelations, to preserve that dignity and sublimity of style which might seem not unworthy of the majesty of that Being whom he gave out to be the Author of them, and to imitate the prophetic manner of the Old Testament; but he has not neglected even the other arts of oratory, wherein he succeeded so well, and so strangely captivated the minds of his audience, that several of his opponents thought it the effect of witchcraft and enchantment, as he sometimes complains.[46]

As for the translator and commentator, he says on page 70 of his notes:

> Know that we do not deny that the Qur'án is eloquent in some places, but we deny their claim that it is miraculous in its eloquence and that it surpasses the power of mortal men, just as some of their own sects have denied this before us. As for its eloquence in some passages, in the style of the Arabs, it is no wonder that it should be so. For the author was from the tribe of the Quraysh, the most eloquent of the Arab tribes, and, in addition, he spent his childhood among the Sa'd clan, who were just as eloquent as Quraysh. Therefore, he was able to combine the expressiveness and stylistic purity of the nomad with the clarity and splendor of civilized speech. This is what prompted him to boast, "I am the most eloquent of the Arabs, and have been given all words."
>
> Then he spent twenty-three years composing his book. During this time he chose from the speech of his own tribe and that of his wetnurse the highest rhetorical style, selecting their most eloquent terms. He employed them to express whatever came into his mind whenever he was ready. Thus, his book became eloquent in many places. But this by no means requires that it be a miracle—just as the poetry of Zuhayr, the discourses of Qass ibn Sá'idah, and the words of

> Saḥbán are not counted as miracles.* This is the case even though, were they to be compared to the Qur'án in regard to their rhetorical beauty, eloquence, and clarity, they would sometimes surpass it. If the Qur'án were the speech of God Himself, and if God wished to challenge the Arabs with its eloquence, it would have had to be more eloquent than it is, and much better organized. Moreover, it would have had to be purified from the errors, the solecisms, the pallidness, and the other faults of speech it contains, since it would be inappropriate to attribute these to God.

The commentator then goes on to cite many passages in the noble Qur'án which he alleges are incompatible with eloquence and good rhetorical style, rejecting therein what he calls manifold and obvious faults, including errors, solecisms, and pallor of style. He cites weak analogies, fragmentary sentences, and ineloquent prolixity which transform such passages into something other than what the speaker intended. He also notes changes in attention from soliloquy to address and from address to soliloquy, the repetition of the same word in a single sentence, inharmony of sounds, stammering, corrupt meanings, and so forth. Were an investigator of the truth to look closely at his criticisms, he would see that only the Throne Verse has escaped the darts of his refutation and detraction.† He did confess the sublime eloquence of this noble verse, lest it be said of him that he is altogether ignorant of eloquence and rhetoric or that bias and fanaticism have completely blinded him.

*Zuhayr, Ibn Sá'idah, and Saḥbán were early Arab literary figures.

†Qur'án 2:255. This verse is noted for its particularly majestic beauty.

These doubts will certainly deceive many among those with weak reason and incline those with ailing hearts from the truth. For people by nature wish to curry favor with the victorious party, to incline toward false doubts, and endeavor to flatter those with standing and ephemeral sovereignty. How often do we see among the present generation that a youth, a scion of the Arabs, will affect foreign words and other barbarisms in his speech, corrupting his accent in imitation of Westerners. He seeks only to mimic the proponents of modern civilization and to flatter the powerful. However, this doubt and skepticism has resulted solely from the deviation of the interpreters of the Qur'án from the straight path in explaining how the Qur'án is irrefutable, and in interpreting its verses. Had the religious scholars established its truth in accordance with this path, and so interpreted its verses, the matter would not have led to foolish discussions and cold criticisms.

This is because, as we pointed out above, eloquence and rhetorical beauty are hidden, mysterious, and subtle characteristics about which tastes differ and opinions and views multiply. These traits easily lend themselves to controversy and distortion so that doubts about them become stamped on simple hearts and weak minds. This is particularly so where this process is abetted by religious emotions, nationalistic ties, and kinship solidarity. How few are those who truly recognize rhetorical beauty in exposition or eloquence of speech—even among proficient litterateurs and bearers of the pen! Otherwise, every writer would be an eloquent author and every speaker a gifted and articulate orator. The professionals do not find this an easy matter to discuss, and the weak do not find it easy to accept.

However, the Prophet, through the revelation of

the Qur'án to him, did undeniably demonstrate a knowledge and power that allowed him to guide nations, to root out the maladies afflicting the world's peoples, to found an inspired law and to raise up an Islamic nation—in spite of the opposition of other great nations and religions. All this is obvious and tangible, such that little dispute is possible and all attempts at distortion are useless. Who can deny that the great nations—the Arabs, Iranians, Gílánís, Turks, Indians, Chinese, and the inhabitants of Africa—forsook the darkness of idol worship and fire worship? Or that they ceased rejecting the prophets and entered into the light of monotheism, the worship of God alone, and faith in His prophets, messengers, angels, and Holy Books?

Before the revelation of the Qur'án these nations worshiped fire and idols; they did not know of Moses or of Jesus or the other prophets. These great nations found guidance, believed, and surrendered themselves to God because of the first Muslims. These Muslims were created by Islam, and Islam was legislated and founded by the Prophet. Finally, Muḥammad became a prophet only because the glorious Qur'án was revealed to him. This is the secret of the words which God used to confound the haughty deniers: "Bring a book from God that gives better guidance than these, and follow it, if you speak truly."[47]

Yes, it is true that Muslims have often been accused of spreading Islam by the sword and establishing it by force rather than by allowing people free choice and convincing them with proofs. We have rebutted and answered these charges previously, and we shall repeat our argument here so as to fulfill our purpose and confirm the hearts. If we leaf through the histories of Islamic nations, pursuing their traces and searching their annals, we find not the least indication that the Prophet, or the caliphs, or the kings of Islam ever compelled any nation to embrace Islam. Rather, we witness the very opposite. For instance, it is recorded that the Umayyad caliphs and the Marwánid princes (who are the ones intended by the Holy Books when they speak of the terrible Behemoth and the Beast which emerges from the pit),[48] forbade anyone to enter Islam because they desired to increase their income from levies on non-Muslims and they feared that through conversions they would forfeit tax revenues. This was owing to their greed in piling up riches and their desire to spread their wealth on vile passions and base pleasures. 'Umar ibn 'Abdu'l-'Azíz, that king known in the books as abstemious and just, even wrote to one of his generals censuring him for preventing people from entering Islam.* He wrote, "Muḥammad—peace be upon him—was sent as a guide, not as a tax collector!" This should inform the reasoning person of the manner in which Islam spread. It relieves us of any need to search further or digress at length on this theme.

As for Christianity, while we believe that it is a divinely inspired religion and a divine revelation, if we page through its chronicles and follow its development, we find that its history is stained with gore. Its annals contain the most horrifying instances of nations forced to follow this religion through killing and burning people alive. How much blood they shed; how many persons they burned; how many women and children they left widows and orphans! They exterminated nations and massacred peoples—all as a means of propagating the Trinity and rendering the Cross vic-

*'Umar II (r. 717–720 A.D.), the son of 'Abdu'l-'Azíz, one of the few truly pious caliphs of the Umayyad dynasty, treated minorities well and encouraged voluntary conversion to Islam.

torious! Anyone who wishes to read further about all this may peruse the history of the church by the American scholar James Murdock, published here in Cairo.[49]

What we see today of the way they spread their religion obviates any further need to delve into and investigate the past. The domes of this religion's glory in our own time rest on three pillars: the machinations of ambassadors, the artillery of soldiers, and the gifts of supporters. Of course, we know that the holy teachings of Christianity can, in themselves, dispense with these means, that the glad tidings of the glorious gospel are purified in their essence above these disastrous tools. However, when a person's foot strays from the true path and his eyes wander from the vision of the truth, he does not see the power of the Word of God, ignores the light of His prophecies, and does not recognize that God stands in no need of others. He cleaves to every falsehood and seeks the aid of ephemeral factors. So, let us leave these helpers of religion to dazzle the people's minds with dumdum rifles and Maxime artillery, and proceed to fulfill our pledge to rebut their criticisms of the Qur'án.

We have made it clear that we believe that the Qur'án constitutes a universal proof and an outstanding miracle, owing to the power and guidance God has reposited therein, and that this does not contradict our belief that it is also inimitable in regard to its eloquence and rhetorical beauty. For we have established that the Manifestations of the Cause of God generally, and the blessed Lote-Tree, the Primal Word, in particular, excel all others in the attributes of honor and of perfection—such as knowledge, forebearance, wisdom, courage, patience, determination, resoluteness, and so forth. Likewise they excel others in the beauty of their form, the erectness of their bearing, the excellence of their utterance, and the eloquence of their speech. No one can compare to them in any attribute; no one resembles them in any characteristic. All that is implied here is that not every person can perceive these qualities, that they cannot be seen in all places, nor can they reach every generation, such that they could constitute a comprehensive proof and universal miracle.

This being the case, it is necessary that we fulfill our pledge to make some observations on what this English scholar has written concerning the eloquence of the Qur'án, and to disprove his allegations and delusions about the reason for its spread and influence among nations and religions. We proceed, trusting in God, the Succorer.

The author of this essay on Islam said: "The style of the Qur'án is generally beautiful and fluent, especially where it imitates the prophetic manner and Scripture phrases. It is concise and often obscure. . . ."

We say in reply: he implies that the style of the Qur'án is not beautiful and fluent in some places. However, with typical English cleverness, he has neglected to specify those passages, referring to them only in general. No doubt he realized that he would encounter difficulties from men of the pen, partisans of truth, servants of knowledge, guardians of oratory and writing, and supporters of eloquence and rhetoric. However, this unfortunate Syrian has fallen in with him and has singled out some of these alleged passages, so that it has become necessary to publicly expose him, as we shall clarify, God willing. Then Sale goes on to intimate that the style of the Qur'án in praising and lauding God, His bounties, and His blessings, is somehow borrowed from the Old Testament, and that the Prophet Muḥammad copied it from the prophets of Israel.

We shall not refute his false charges with what was revealed in the Qur'án, where God said, "Had he invented against Us any sayings, We would have seized him by the right hand, then We would surely have cut his life-vein and not one of you could have defended him."[50] Nor shall we cite the fourteenth chapter of Ezekiel wherein the glorious Lord said, "And if the prophet be deceived and speak a word, I, the Lord have deceived that prophet, and will stretch out my hand against him, and will destroy him from the midst of my people Israel."[51] For the scope of God's power, His ability to do His will, His victoriousness, and His invincibility are beyond His servants. Those with dull vision cannot see His omniscience nor His omnipresence among His creatures. Those of clouded sight cannot perceive it, nor can hearts occupied with their natural desires understand it. For this reason only the learned fear Him, only the discerning dread His sovereignty, and only the ignorant and foolish feel safe from His retribution. It is obvious that the arrogant ones of this age must consider the will of God, His volition, His omnipresence and power as nothing.

Indeed, were a person to heed such doubts, he would be forced to reject all the prophets as false, to abandon all the great religions, and to return to idol worship, or to an even more primitive barbarism. For the Christians assert that Muḥammad falsely attributed the Qur'án to God and claim that he borrowed from the Gospel. Likewise, the Jews claim that Jesus copied his teachings from the books of the Old Testament prophets. The Zoroastrians believe that Moses and the prophets of Israel compiled their books from passages borrowed from the ancient Persian prophets. And the Sabians allege that all the later religions have plundered the heritage of antiquity and have plagiarized the excellence of the ancients.

A Zoroastrian leader said in *Sudrih va kushtí*, "David the blacksmith took his words of praise and glorification, and expressions of the unity and oneness of God from the Zend Avesta. He mixed them with songs he copied from Persian masters and pieced them together into psalms, which he distributed to the common people of Israel." It is thus apparent that modern men make the same arguments in rejecting the Manifestations of the Cause of God as did the ancients, and they walk the same path as their predecessors. A rational person devoted to investigation of the truth will not give any weight to the allegations of one religious community about another, unless there is good reason. As the prudent know, however, there is no good reason.

If someone can doubt the Qur'án because of the possibility that the Prophet may have copied the books of the Old Testament prophets, because these books attribute the same characteristics to God as does the Qur'án, then why not doubt the Gospel, since all its teachings can be found in the Book of Confucius, the prophet of the great Chinese nation and the legislator for Chinese "Buddhism"?* This is what we meant when we said that embracing this skepticism can only

*Abu'l-Faḍl has earlier made clear that by "Buddhism" he means the syncretic religion of China, which mixed Confucianism, Buddhism, and Taoism. The legalist element in this syncretism was provided by Confucianism.

lead back to paganism. Indeed, it would raze the edifices of all religions. Is there any religion whose founder did not attribute to God such splendid characteristics as uniqueness, unity, glory, wisdom, power, might, and so forth?

But, in any case, what resemblance is there between the purification and sanctification that God taught in the Qur'án and the anthropomorphic and material characteristics the prophets of Israel ascribed to God? Does it say in the Qur'án that the Lord appeared as a stormy wind in the midst of which appeared the likeness of four living creatures, each with four faces and four wings, whose legs were straight and the soles of whose feet were like the soles of a calf's foot; and who sparkled like burnished bronze? Yet Ezekiel so describes the Lord in the beginning of his book. Or does it say in the Qur'án that the Lord appeared as a rod of almond, as is mentioned in the beginning of the Book of Jeremiah? Does the Qur'án describe the Lord as appearing seated upon a throne, high and lifted up, His train filling the temple; with seraphim standing above Him, each with six wings, so that with two He covered His face, and with two He covered His feet, and with two He flew? Yet so it is mentioned in the sixth chapter of the Book of Isaiah.[52]

There are many more such examples. We have not said this in order to disparage the Holy Books, or to detract from their high station. God forbid! For we have affirmed above our belief in the need to accept the portion of them that is inspired. Rather, our intent is to demonstrate that there is no resemblance or similarity between them and the Qur'án, as that scholar has pretended—as have other writers of attacks and refutations, and other proponents of skepticism and denial.

The most amazing thing that strikes anyone with insight about the works of these deniers is that their objections contradict one another and their grounds for doubt come into conflict. For instance, the Austrian writer Pfander rejected the Qur'án in his book *The Balance of Truth* because he said it did not resemble the books of the prophets of Israel in its glorification and praise of God, and in its predictions and tidings. Yet this erudite Englishman has rejected it because it follows their example and replicates their style. Praise be to Him who has given us minds and characters, and who has distinguished between perceptions and understandings.

The English author goes on to say:

> Though it be written in prose, yet the sentences generally conclude in a long continued rhyme, for the sake of which the sense is often interrupted, and unnecessary repetitions too frequently made, which appear still more ridiculous in a translation, where the ornament, such as it is, for whose sake they were made, cannot be perceived. However, the Arabians are so mightily delighted with this jingling, that they employ it in their most elaborate compositions, which they also embellish with frequent passages of, and allusions to, the Qur'án, so that it is next to impossible to understand them without being well versed in this book.

We have often seen that English writers reproach the people of the East for employing rhetoric, and for their approval of ornamentation in their phrases, harmony in their words, and rhymed prose in their sentences. It is as if observing meter in the flow of speech, and beautifying it with such rhetorical arts as harmony, adornment, and rhymed prose were an unpardonable crime or an unforgivable sin. In reality, this is a sick opinion and a denial of the truth. Indeed, it is nothing less than a distortion and a delusion. I cannot imagine why they appreciate organization, harmony, and rhythm in their buildings and manufactured products but not in works and creations that will last for ages and epochs. They admire it in their edifices, their bridges, and great arches, and even in manufactured items and trivial products such as clothing, shoes, belts, and so forth. The latter wear out and disappear in a year or two.

They demonstrate the utmost versatility in perfecting and beautifying their manufactures, in harmonizing the buttons and adjusting the corners, showing the greatest interest in such things. Since this is the case with them in regard to ephemeral manufactures and trivial occupations, why do they not allow the people of the East to employ harmony, ornamentation, rhymed prose, and embellishment in speech and utterance? For the latter is mankind's highest merit and loftiest attribute. In this human beings excel all other species of animal, and through this books are composed, religious and scientific writings are preserved and transmitted, and rational virtues are maintained forever. By the medium of speech, characters and behavior are refined and human beings are adorned with precious characteristics and dispositions. Is not their stance, then, one of outrageous extremism and detestable misrepresentation?

This empty reproach and hollow censure derives solely from the deficiencies of their own language, which is devoid of delicateness and fluency. The science of rhetoric is a geometry of speech, just as the knowledge of planes and their relation to one another constitutes the geometry of bodies. A writer or an orator must achieve insight into harmony and organization; he must know where to employ ornament and rhymed prose, and where to use metaphors and similes. Otherwise, he will fail to convey his meaning, his composition will be ruined, his speech will lose its elegance, and the benefit of his exposition will be lost. In the same way, a craftsman must have insight into how to organize the constituent parts of his product so it will be graceful and acceptable in form.

We have often written that rhetorical embellishments of speech are like salt on food: a little benefits it, but a great deal ruins it. Eloquence in speech is like natural beauty in a human being. For true eloquence consists only of ordering the parts of speech beautifully and choosing appropriate words, just as natural beauty in a human being lies simply in an erect stature and limbs of proper proportions. To decorate speech with rhetorical adornments is like adorning a person with jewels and clothing. If one lacks inherent good character, outward embellishments cannot beautify him. In the same way, should someone go to extremes in his clothing, his natural beauty and erect stature will be veiled from view.

For this reason, the elegance, delicateness, grace, beauty of style, and perfection of composition of al-Ḥarírí, al-Hamadání, al-Khwarazmí, and other masters of exposition does not equal that of the discourses and letters of 'Alí ibn Abí Ṭálib, the Commander of the Faithful, or of the other imams and caliphs.[53] This is so in spite of the fact that the expressions employed by al-Ḥarírí and Badí'u'z-Zamán[54] are more crafted, contain more rhymed prose, and have a more perfect rhythm. For they were composed with affectation, contemplation, deliberation and precision, in contrast to the discourses of the imáms. These latter came naturally and extemporaneously, without the mannerisms, forethought, deliberation, and meditation which are normal among authors. For this reason they say, "Nature prevails." There is the same relation between the revealed Word of God and the discourses of the imáms, for the Qur'án is even more graceful, delicate, and sweet, as the wise can plainly see.

The writer's false impression that the sense of the verses is interrupted for the sake of the rhyme derives from his ignorance of that sense, for he has already complained that the verses are "concise and often obscure." It is not only in the glorious Qur'án that the meanings of the holy verses are difficult to grasp and remain remote from the understanding of laymen. The words of all the prophets are difficult, perplexing, obscure, concealed, and inaccessible to inconstant hearts, and they remain distant from weak minds. Whoever seeks their meaning must be disappointed, until the advent of a terrible and mighty Day. Whoever endeavors to interpret them before the All-Merciful, the Compassionate, unseals them must go astray.

We have seen recorded in the books of the Old Testament prophets the words of God, the Most High: "I desire to open my mouth in parables and to speak of things concealed since the foundation of the world."[55] Were the meanings of the words of God clear, obvious, and easily comprehended, such that any remote one could comprehend them and any fool could grasp them, then nothing would be concealed that God might open His mouth in parables, or His prophets might seal it in former ages and generations.[56]

The best evidence that the verses of the Holy Scriptures are not easy to understand is that the scholars among the Jews have agreed that the prophecies of the Old Testament did not apply to Jesus, and indeed, they take them as the strongest grounds for denying him. However, the scholars of the Christian community are unanimous in their judgment that these predictions do perfectly apply to his appearance, and they have made these prophecies the foundation of their affirmation of his truth. Is this not the most obvious proof, the strongest evidence, that the words of the prophets are often obscure, difficult, and perplexing?

The Jewish scholars allege that they take the interpretation of their books from the Fathers of the tradition, that it has been passed from elder to elder, and been preserved from generation to generation. And who are the Fathers of tradition? They are the great prophets—Isaiah, Jeremiah, Zechariah, and the others. But the truth of the matter is that the Jewish community has proved itself ignorant of the meaning of the glad tidings of the Old Testament. For this reason, they rejected Jesus, while the Christians followed him. And the Muslims have followed in their tracks, as the prophetic tradition attests: "Follow the pathways of those who preceded you, inch by inch and cubit by cubit."

The writer continues:

> It is probable the harmony of expression which the Arabians find in the Qur'án might contribute not a little to make them relish the doctrine therein taught, and give an efficacy to arguments which, had they been nakedly proposed without this rhetorical dress, might not have so easily prevailed. Very extraodinary effects

> are related of the power of words well chosen and artfully placed, which are no less powerful either to ravish or amaze than music itself; wherefore as much has been ascribed by the best orators to this part of rhetoric as to any other. He must have a very bad ear who is not uncommonly moved with the very cadence of a well-turned sentence; and Muḥammad seems not to have been ignorant of the enthusiastic operation of rhetoric on the minds of men; for which reason he has not only employed his utmost skill in these his pretend revelations, to preserve that dignity and sublimity of style which might seem not unworthy of the majesty of that Being whom he gave out to be the Author of them, and to imitate the prophetic manner of the Old Testament; but he has not neglected even the other arts of oratory, wherein he succeeded so well, and so strangely captivated the minds of his audience, that several of his opponents thought it the effect of witchcraft and enchantment, as he sometimes complains.

It is clear to people of knowledge that every one of the blessed, exalted virtues and gifts—such as glory, wealth, authority, sovereignty, knowledge, erudition, eloquence, rhetorical excellence, beauty of voice and exposition, and so forth—whereby commands can be implemented and to which hearts are attracted, possesses a perspicuous power and an irresistible force. These virtues exercise a clear influence. However, it is not rationally tenable to suppose that the potency of this influence could ever reach the point that it could create a new religion or an independent religious community that continues to exist for centuries and ages without the permission of God. Otherwise, the proof of true religion would be undermined, the path to knowledge of the divine laws would be concealed, the beacon of Eternal Truth would be extinguished, and the standards of guidance would be pulled down. There would be no distinction between truth and falsehood, guidance and deception, and no criterion that would divide true counsel from error, or right direction from temptation.

We have earlier explained the degree to which miracles provide conclusive evidence or proof, and we have established by clear proofs that they do not constitute complete or independent evidence for the truth of anyone's claims or for the validity of the law he might ordain. For this reason, Christ and Muḥammad refused to respond to requests for wonders, or to give comfort to those who suggested miracles, as the verses of the Gospel and the Qur'án bear witness. All nations are alike in claiming miracles for the ordainers of their religions and ascribing wonders to the founders of their faiths, and even to the masters of their mystical orders and the originators of their schools of law. They go even further, attributing extraordinary powers to the tombs of their saints!

However, God has provided unambiguous signs to distinguish the truth. He has erected for it an eternal beacon and ordained for it unfailing tokens and emblems. The greatest and most conspicuous of these is that heavenly power wherein no soul shares, and that divine force the like of which no one can produce —power to promulgate a unique Message and found a new religion. This is the only power that can withstand the onslaught of all the peoples of the world, the resistance and opposition of the combined might of the princes and ecclesiastics of the East and the West, and finally overcome them. For the trait of loving one's old familiar religion is deeply ingrained in the people's hearts, and the disposition to hate a new and innovative creed is well known in the unjust and the haughty.

Christ spoke of this heavenly power when he said, "They will see the Son of Man coming on the clouds of heaven with power and great glory."[57] And in the Mother Book, it is recorded, "Should they hide me away in the depths of the earth, yet would they find Me riding aloft on the clouds."[58] It was to this that the glorious Qur'án alluded when God said, "Our host —they are the victors."[59] Let us suppose that this clear proof failed and was disregarded as a result of weak and unfounded doubts. How then would the validity of the prophets be established? How would we distinguish between truth and falsehood, between the enduring and the transient? Once this has been understood, the reader will realize the fallacy of the English writer's fanciful suggestion that the Arabs might have accepted the Qur'án because of the eloquence of its verses and the elegance of its style.

He goes on to insist that, "He must have a very bad ear who is not uncommonly moved with the cadence of a well-turned sentence." It has escaped him that raising such doubts wreaks a greater harm upon his own religion than upon any other and breaches the bulwarks of Christianity before those of Islam. For the Jews accuse Christians of having dazzled the minds of simple people with worldly trinkets of gold and silver when this faith first arose in Asia and Europe. Surely shining silver and glittering bullion are more likely to attract and deceive than the cadence of a well-turned sentence or a moving song! This is especially so if false-hearted people contrive some marvel that startles the hearts of the uneducated and agitates the souls of the simple. Consult the fifth chapter of the Acts of the Apostles if you would see signs and wonders such as enchanted minds and enthralled hearts.[60] The English in particular are knowledgeable concerning the people's love of money and the effect if has upon the soul, a motivation that far exceeds by comparison any influence which phrases and melodies might exert.

Should such unfounded skepticism be taken seriously, it would not stop with Islam. Say: "Peace be upon all the religions!"

It is true that fortune, power, authority, discourse, poetry, song, and melody all exercise undeniable influence and act in ways that the eye can see. However, those who denied the Qur'án amply possessed all these advantages. In fact, their influence in ensuring that the people would continue to practice their original religion and inherited faith was more powerful and more easily exerted. Among the Arabs who rejected the mission of the Prophet Muḥammad, warring on him and declaring their enmity toward him, were Abú Jahl, Abú Sufyán ibn Ḥarb, 'Utbah and Shaybah—the two sons of Rabí'ah, Naḍr ibn al-Ḥárith, and so on. These were all stentorian orators, renowned for their eloquence; their names are immortalized in the texts of books and the pages of history.

If eloquence and rhetoric were so influential and powerful, would not these fluent tongues, eloquent discourses, balanced phrases, and moving melodies have served to maintain the Arabs in their ancient religion? For continuing to practice the old religion would have been easier for them than embracing a new Faith which they had not inherited and following a strange and unfamiliar path. Is this not because the power of God surpasses their power and the will of God transcends their will? For ordinary causes are confounded by celestial ones.

Moreover, religions do not come into being because minds are beguiled or hearts captivated. The writer's Syrian colleague, after all, has clearly stated that there are in the Qur'án many lapses of eloquence. It is very nearly only the Throne Verse that escapes the barbs of his refutations and objections. Where, then, is this eloquence that enthralled the Arabs? The Syrian commentator has said that Muḥammad's opponents saw nothing miraculous about this "miracle" (that is, the Qur'án). Thus they rejected it, and they were eloquent Arabs. He also asserts that the poetry of Zuhayr, the discourses of Qass ibn Sá'idah, and the words of Saḥbán are not reckoned as miracles, even though they far surpass the Qur'án in rhetorical beauty, eloquence, and clarity.

He says: "If the Qur'án were the speech of God Himself, and if God wished to challenge the Arabs with its eloquence, it would have had to be more eloquent than it is, and much better organized. Moreover, it would have had to be purified from the errors, the solecisms, pallidness, and the other faults of speech it contains. . . ." Thus, the Syrian commentator has pulled down the structure erected by his English mentor in his discourse. For, by the Life of God, it is unimaginable that the Arab nation, which possessed poets and orators of undeniable eloquence and rhetorical ability such as Qass and Zuhayr, who, he claims, surpassed the Qur'án, could have been captivated and enthralled by this Book if it contained all the unconcealed pallidness, solecisms, and errors he imagines.

If the Qur'án had achieved such a rank in the hierarchy of eloquence and rhetorical excellence that it had astonished the most eloquent men among the Arabs and rendered them unable to resist it, so that they cast off the robe of their original religion and donned the vestments of the new Islamic revelation, then this would have proved the soundness of Muslim scholars' assertions that the eloquence and rhetorical beauty of the Qur'án transcend mortal abilities. But if the Qur'án's eloquence and rhetoric did not surpass that of other Arabs, then this would establish the falsity of the English scholar's claim that Muḥammad beguiled the hearts of the Arab nation with verbal ornaments and well-ordered verses. It would then be demonstrated that this noble Scripture, this ancient Word, vanquished the people of the world solely by divine power and celestial potency, and not by harmonious words and rhymed phrases.

It is difficult to refrain from bursting into laughter at the clever Syrian's statement that "Muḥammad's opponents did not see anything miraculous in this 'miracle' and rejected it." Have the enemies of any of the prophets ever seen anything miraculous in their miracles, have they ever failed to reject them? Does not the Jewish community, the nearest of all peoples to Christ, reject all his miracles after the expiration of more than eighteen centuries? Is it really permissible for learned men to allow their religious feelings, their ignorant fanaticism, to overcome them to the extent that they forget reason and moderation and object to the founder of Islam with arguments from which no prophet in previous centuries and generations has ever been immune?

We direct the attention of the insightful to the French Revolution, in 1792 A.D. The spirit of liberty had grown within the French philosophers, and they rose to overthrow absolute and dictatorial authority.

They were determined to reject obscure, inherited dogmas. They maintained that it was impossible for European peoples to retain the Christian dogmas they once embraced, after they had made such progress in natural science, mathematics, and astronomy. Therefore, these thinkers wished to create a religion whose basic beliefs and moral laws would be simpler and more easily accepted by the reason and the mind than the ancient dogmas which sound judgment and undeviating reason must reject and dismiss.

They therefore founded a religion based on the worship of God alone, and made churches the places of this worship. Their articles of faith were simple and they contained two major propositions: the first was the recognition of the Creator's existence, and the second was the acceptance of the immortality of the soul—that is, its continuance as a perceiving, self-subsisting entity after death. Their moral laws were also grounded in two major principles: the first was the love of God, and the second was the love of mankind. They included in their rituals, which were created by some philosophers, obligatory prayers and the commemoration and praise of God. They also established in their religion other simple practices, such as placing platters of fruit and fragrant plants on an altar and using vocal and instrumental music in their gatherings.

After they had established the fundamentals of this religion, agreed on them, and grounded them on what they thought were firm foundations, the minister of the interior appointed a group of great writers and orators and sent them to all the provinces of France. Their task was to call the people to accept this new religion. They spared no effort to introduce their religion into every French city, and their ideals even spread to other countries. Nawfal ibn Ni'matu'lláh of

Tripoli said in his book *The Choicest of Volumes on Touring Learning,*[61] after describing this incident, "Some persons in Paris and elsewhere adopted this religion, but most paid no attention to them. After a short while, they became extinct and all news of them ceased."[62]

If the effect of eloquence, rhetoric, harmony of words, and rhymed phrases on mortal minds were so great as to induce their acceptance of a false religion, such that they would yield to and obey an artificial religious law, then would not the eloquence and rhetoric of these eminent men have proven effective in promulgating the religion they had fashioned with their noble minds and the power of their philosophy? Among them were great authors and leading orators renowned for the magic of their words, the vigor of their pens, the fluency of their tongues, and the sweetness of their phrases. They were the peers of Voltaire and Jean-Jacques Rousseau. They employed reason, planning, knowledge, erudition, eloquence, and rhetoric. They used temporal power, sovereignty, wealth, and music to diffuse this religion which, they claimed, had been created by the most august minds of mankind, including among them geniuses, eminent philosophers and lights of the age—such as one generation seldom produces. A multitude of military commanders and civil leaders obeyed them, and they achieved the utmost success in transforming dictatorial authority into constitutional government.

However, God demonstrated their impotence, led their efforts astray, disappointed their hopes, and dispersed them, in the realm of religion. For the foundation and the endurance of any religion pertains solely to His will and depends on His permission and volition, not on other means or causes. God thus made apparent the weakness of their knowledge, the inferiority of their understanding, the folly of their reason, and the limitation of their intelligence. For they claimed that religions could be created by human minds, and that worldly means could be employed to propagate and promote them. God thus thwarted their pride, destroyed their power, broke their backs, effaced their labors, encompassed them with His strength and perfection, and besieged them with His power and vengeance. For they planned to found a religion without His leave and endeavored to create a religious law without first determining His will. The stories of Arghún Khán, the Mongol; and Sa'du'd-Dawlah, the Jew, in Iran; 'Alá'u'd-Dín al-Khaljí in India; and the French philosophers in Europe contain a lesson for those of insight and a reminder and an admonition to the People of the Book.[63]

We have said above that raising such doubts would lead one to doubt all the prophets and would end in the destruction of all religions. The reason for this is obvious to anyone familiar with rational proofs and logical analogies. It is a fact that a rational proposition contained in a premise is universal and will not admit to limitations. Naturally, a rational proposition is valid for all its particulars, and a universal must apply to all its components. The reason instinctively senses this relationship. It cannot be prevented from instinctively realizing this by extraneous impediments such as love, hate, communal or racial solidarity, and so forth. For the latter are extraneous to the essence of the question. The reason will, by deliberating on it, notice the universal applicability of a proposition whether or not these impediments exist.

Thus if a doubt develops about the truth of the Islamic religion on the grounds that the founder of that religion may have imprinted his thoughts on the people's minds by the glibness of his tongue and the rhetorical beauty of his exposition; and if reason finds the proposition that false religions can spread merely through eloquent speech and magical utterance a tenable one, then this doubt will rationally follow in regard to the ordainers of previous religions. The reason will doubt that these religions did not also employ this power, or some other means, to promulgate their views and imprint their thoughts on the innocent hearts and simple minds of fishermen and shepherds.

The longer ago the founder lived, the stronger this skepticism will grow. For doubt will only be strengthened by the obscurity of ancient history, the depths of whose darkness even the sharpest eyes cannot penetrate. Those ages are remote and their beginnings have been obliterated. The number of intervening generations is great, and the accumulation over time of ambiguities is tremendous. For this reason, it is a difficult and imposing task to establish historically the existence of the founders of some of these ancient religions, much less the means they adopted to propagate their religions and promote their views.

By the Life of God! If anyone were permitted to doubt the Holy Book of Islam, which is the furthest thing from sorcery (or to impugn the medium of speech, which is the noblest trait of humankind) on the basis of a suspicion that its revealer enchanted the minds of the people with it, then how much more appropriate would it be to question the wonders they have ascribed to their own prophets! For these wonders are in the same class as the alleged sorcery: there is a clear and obvious similarity between them. Did the

English scholar think that the philosophers of Egypt, who ascribed Moses' miracles to legerdemain and sorcery, were any less discerning or perceptive than he and his like? Westerners set out every year from Europe and America to see the awesome works of the Egyptians, works that attest to the breadth of their knowledge and the elevation of their thought. They undergo fearful hardships and spend their money to visit these astonishing Pharaonic ruins, which bespeak sublime perception and subtle discernment.

Belief in sorcery, in the sense intended by the common people, is simply a remnant of superstitions of the Dark Ages. These veils have been rent by the light of the dawning sun of knowledge, and this accumulated gloom has been dispelled by the rising luminary of truth. In reality, "sorcery" denotes the same thing as "falsehood," as the oral reports of the imams of the House of the Prophet, collected in the book *Oceans of Light,* indicate.[64] Every people that denies the truth of a messenger's mission must attribute his signs and tokens to trickery, rather than to reality. This was the case with the pre-Judaic religions in their repudiation of Moses, the Jews in their rejection of Jesus, the Christians in their spurning of the Prophet Muḥammad, and so on. God bestowed upon the imams of the Prophet's House the station of "guardianship," which is equivalent to the prophethood of the prophets of Israel, as the Prophet's saying demonstrates: "The learned of my community are like the prophets of the children of Israel, or better than the prophets of Israel." But aside from this, they were from the line of the Arabs and from their most elite tribes. They were, therefore, more knowledgeable about the ways to use the words of the Arabic language, and about their true meanings, than the interlopers and strangers who intruded upon it after ages had worn it down and the revolution of centuries had obscured its peculiar traits and origins.

From the preceding it can be concluded that when the English scholar opens the door to such doubts, they will subvert the pillars of his own religion, in whose soundness he believes, before they will harm other religions. Thus, one can see that such skepticism as this has harmed the sacred Christian faith more than it has the holy revelation of Islam. For materialistic schools have blossomed and multiplied among the Christians, including Darwinists, socialists, and anarchists—groups that deny all the prophets and deride all religions. Even the great minds of Europe have grown apprehensive at the growth of these groups, and their rapid advance has alarmed them.

This is indicated by what one such thinker said to the renowned Prime Minister Gladstone when he noticed that the latter was anxious about the future of his people.* He asked him, "Is it that you fear the tremendous progress of science will subvert the foundations of theology, which is the basis of human society?"

It is also demonstrated by what the famous priest Loyson, the French orator, said in his discourse at the Khedive's playhouse to an audience of more than two thousand eminent Muslims and Christians.[65] These included great religious scholars and princes, consuls from various countries, and the intelligentsia of Egypt.

*William E. Gladstone (1809–1898) was the greatest British statesman of the nineteenth century. He was a liberal and a humanitarian who served as prime minister four times between 1868 and 1894.

This renowned orator said in the course of his address:

> Two monuments in Egypt have astonished me for a reason not found in the tombs and temples of the Pharaohs: these are the Azhar University and the statue of Ibráhím.* For these two point to the future, while the former speak of the past. The Azhar University, with its tens of thousands of students studying religious sciences, arriving from the furthest realms between Morocco and China, is fit to quicken the Islamic world. Safeguard it! Safeguard it! For it upholds the Word of God, which has now begun to fade from the horizons of Europe. It is to be feared that, should this Word vanish altogether, we shall fall into a savagery more bestial than that of the most contemptible barbarians.

No wonder alarm and dread have seized the hearts of such men as Loyson and Gladstone's questioner, who are concerned with the future of their people. For they see with their own eyes that every year the schools of Europe graduate a huge army of youths girded with the sword of natural sciences and armed with the weapon of Darwinist ideology, assaulting religious beliefs, mocking the divine laws, deriding the Holy Scriptures, and belittling all spiritual authority. They are unable to find any escape from the circle of their sciences and acquired knowledge. Their principles and foundations are all established through con-

*Ibráhím Pasha (1789–1848) was the eldest son of Egyptian Viceroy Muḥammad-'Alí. He was one of modern Egypt's great fighting men, leading campaigns in Arabia, Greece, Palestine, Syria, and Anatolia.

clusive empirical proofs. They know of no way to apply and adjust them to the contents of the Holy Scriptures. For these are replete with sealed, prophetic symbols and allusions, and mysterious, concealed enigmas and metaphors.

For instance, an astronomer knows by proofs the truth of the spheres circling in space: that they are infinite in every direction, that these are suns fixed in their positions about which revolve planets about which, in turn, revolve moons. He knows that suns are not solid, translucent bodies, and they are not subject to being rent or welded together. How can he then confess the truth of the statements in the Torah, the Gospel, and the Qur'án that the sky will be cleft asunder, shaken, rolled up, and completely transformed? How can he believe that the heavens and the earth will be made new, their elements consumed in fire? Or that the sun and moon will fail to give their light, that the planets will be scattered upon the earth, that it is possible for a man to ascend into heaven and descend from it, and so forth? All this is entirely contrary to the established principles of the astronomical and natural sciences. Such a one will fail to recognize anything in these words revealed in the sacred scriptures save their literal sense. It will never occur to him that perhaps these words possess meanings of which he is ignorant, realities of which he is heedless, as is mentioned in the heavenly books and openly stated in the words of the prophets.

The European peoples generally, and the English in particular, contain within themselves many virtuous, erudite, noble, and religious persons. However, the demands of progress and the rapid advance of the natural sciences when compared to their feeble and confused theology leads inevitably to the downfall of the virtuous and the triumph of the materialists. At that point, a faction characterized by coarseness and hardness of heart seats itself upon the dais of authority and leadership. This is owing to the eclipse of the fear of God within their hearts, which are not softened by His mention. They thus commit every sin and forbidden act in the name of civilization, just as Eastern potentates used to do before them. They cause the collapse of society and undermine the foundations of religion and true humanity, as Gladstone's questioner pointed out and Loyson mentioned in his speech.

What we have said up to this point demonstrates that these skeptics have created a breach in the bulwark of religion, of civilization, and of humanity such as can be filled only by that which God promised in the Holy Books concerning the renewal of mankind, the alteration in the heavens, the illumination of the earth with the light of her Lord, and the banishment of the first gloom. The portents of these irrevocable promises are manifest, their harbingers have appeared, their day has arrived, and their time has come, if only there were hearts to perceive their significance and understand their meaning.

We shall close our response to the erudite critic by reciting the wise Remembrance, wherein the All-Glorious, the All-Knowing said: "What, have they not journeyed in the land and beheld how was the end of those before them? These were stronger than they in might and left firmer traces in the earth; yet what they acquired did not avail them. So, when their Messengers brought them the clear signs, they rejoiced in such knowledge as they had, and were encompassed by what they mocked at."[66]

We shall here lay down our pen and close the book, imploring God to inspire us with what is best for us and for our brethren in the beginning and in the end. This composition was completed for God, the All-Great, by the pen of this poor author, Abu'l-Faḍl Gulpáygání of Iran, at the beginning of Rabí'ath-Thání 1316 A.H. [1898 A.D.] in Cairo.

Notes

PART I
ANSWERS TO QUESTIONS OF AN INDIAN SCHOLAR

1. Qur'án 86:13–11.

2. The first tradition from the Prophet Muḥammad is given in Averroes, *Kitáb al-kashf ʻan manáhij al-adillah*, ed. Maḥmúd Qásim (Cairo: Anglo-Egyptian Bookstore, 1964), p. 191. The second tradition ("Speak to the people . . .") is cited in Averroes, *On the Harmony of Religion and Philosophy*, trans. George F. Hourani (London: Luzac and Co., 1961), p. 52. Averroes (1122–1198 A.D.), the renowned philosopher of Córdoba, Muslim Spain, was the most eminent follower of Aristotle in medieval Islam. The two works by him mentioned above were reprinted in Cairo in 1895 from the 1859 Munich edition of M.J. Müller, who rediscovered them.

3. Qur'án 10:39.

4. Qur'án 7:53.

5. Qur'án 75:18–19.

6. Qur'án 9:30.

7. Qur'án 3:124–25: "When thou saidst to the believers, 'Is it not enough for you that your Lord should reinforce you with three thousand angels sent down upon you? Yea; if you are patient and godfearing, and the foe come against you instantly, your Lord will reinforce you with five thousand swooping angels'"; Qur'án 8:9: "When you were calling on your Lord for succour and He answered you, 'I shall reinforce you with a thousand angels riding behind you.'"

8. Qur'án 25:7.

9. Naṣíru'd-Dín Ṭúsí, *Tajríd al-i'riqád,* commentary by Muḥammad ash-Shírází (Najaf: Maṭba'at al-Ádáb, 1961), p. 165.

10. Qur'án 38:69.

11. Qur'án 29:45; 2:45.

12. Qur'án 15:99.

13. Qur'án 62:6.

14. This argument is in part directed against the North African philosopher and historian 'Abdu'r-Raḥmán ibn-Khaldun (1332–1406 A.D.). Ibn-Khaldun, who has been called the founder of sociology, argued that a religion can only succeed if it receives the backing of the prophet's people on the basis of kinship solidarity. See ibn-Khaldun, *The Muqaddimah,* 3 vols., trans. Franz Rosenthal (New York: Pantheon Books, 1958) 1:322–27.

15. Qur'án 15:99.

16. See Qur'án 5:115.

17. Qur'án 50:42.

18. The author of the *Ṣiḥáḥ* was Ismá'íl al-Jawharí (d. 1006–7 A.D.), a lexicographer of Arabic from Turkish Central Asia. He studied in Baghdad and made language studies among the bedouin in Syria and Iraq. He finally settled in Nishapur, where he died. He made a monumental contribution to Arabic lexicography through his celebrated dictionary, *Táj al-lughah wa ṣiḥáḥ al-'Arabiyyah* [The crown of the language and Arabic's authentic words], 2 vols., (Buláq: Buláq Press, 1282/1865–66). For this tradition, see vol. 2, s.v. '*K*K.

19. Muḥyi'd-Dín Ibnu'l-'Arabí (1165–1240 A.D.) was one of the greatest Sufi mystics of Islam. He was born in Murcia and grew up in Seville. He was an acquaintance of Averroes, but his metaphysics owed more to Neoplatonism than to peripatetic philosophy. He began his major work, *al-Futúḥát al-Makkiyyah* [Meccan victories] while on pilgrimage to Islam's holy city. After traveling in Iraq, Turkey, and Syria, he settled in Damascus, where he died. He was especially known for his doctrine of *waḥdatu'l-wujúd* (better translated as "existential monism" than as "pantheism"), which held that only God exists in an absolute sense.

Kamálu'd-Dín Muḥammad ibn Ṭalḥah al-'Adawí (1186–1254 A.D.) studied in Nishapur and taught the traditions in Aleppo and Damascus. He was briefly a minister to Al-Málik as-Sa'íd and is said afterwards to have become an ascetic.

20. 'Abdu'l-Wahháb ash-Sha'rání, *al-Yawáqít wa'l-jawáhir fí bayán 'aqá'id al-akábir*, 2 vols., (Beirut: Dár al-Ma'rifah, n.d. [offset of 1899 Cairo ed.]) 2:128. Ash-Sha'rání (1491–1565 A.D.) was a prominent Egyptian mystic. The passage here referred to is quoted from Muḥyi'd-Dín Ibnu'l-'Arabí, *al-Futúḥát al-Makkiyyah*, 4 vols., (Cairo: Dár al-Kutub al-'Arabiyyah al-Kubrá, 1329/1911) 3:327.

PART II
COMMENTARY ON "THEN IT IS OURS TO EXPLAIN IT." (QUR'ÁN 75:19)

1. Qur'án 3:7; 10:39.
2. Qur'án 7:53.
3. Matt. 13:34–35. The quotation is from Ps. 78:2, attributed to Asaph the Seer (2 Chron. 29–30).
4. John 16:12.
5. Yaḥyá ibn Ḥabash as-Suhrawardí, *Hayákil an-núr*, ed. Muḥammad 'Alí Abú Rayyán (Cairo: Grande Librairie Commerciale, 1957), pp. 87–88. Suhrawardí (1152/3-1191 A.D.) was born near Zanján, Iran. He studied peripatetic philosophy and Islamic law in Maraghih and continued his philosophical studies in Isfahan. He then traveled, spending much time in Anatolia, and finally settled in Aleppo, Syria. There, his mixture of philosophy and mysticism became controversial. He was executed for heresy by the government of Ṣaláḥu'd-Dín al-Ayyúbí (the Sunní Muslim leader, better known in the West as Saladin, who defeated the European crusaders and overthrew the Shí'í Fáṭimid dynasty in Egypt). Suhrawardí was charged with believing that God could send a prophet after Muḥammad. This contradicted the Sunní orthodoxy that Muḥammad was the last prophet.

6. Qur'án 29:43; Ps. 78:2.
7. Literally, Paraclete.
8. Paraphrase of various passages in John 14–16; John 14:26.
9. Qur'án 75:19.
10. Qur'án 7:57.
11. Qur'án 5:101.
12. Qur'án 75:16.
13. Qur'án 75:17.
14. Qur'án 75:19.
15. Saḥíḥ al-Bukhárí, vol. 1, with English trans. Muhammad Muhsin Khan (Medina: Islamic University, 1971), p. 5.
16. Qur'án 29:49; 26:193–96.

PART III
THE ALEXANDRIAN EPISTLE: BIBLICAL PROPHECIES ABOUT ISLAM

1. Qur'án 89:22.
2. Quoted from Enoch 1:9.
3. See Qur'án 19:56–57 and 21:85.
4. Matt. 1:1–6; Luke 3:23–38.
5. Muḥammad ibn Isḥáq, *The Life of Muḥammad,* trans. A. Guillaume (Lahore: Oxford University Press, 1974), p. 81.
6. Isa. 63:8–10.
7. Qur'án 17:110.
8. Deut. 32:40.
9. Cf. Rev. 22:13.
10. See Matt. 11:14. Cf. Mal. 4:5.
11. 2 Kings 2:11. Elijah died ca. 849 B.C.
12. Qur'án 54:50; 2:285; 15:75.
13. Qur'án 7:71.
14. Rev. 11:1–19.
15. Qur'án 17:60.
16. Majdu'd-Dín al-Fírúzábádí, *al-Qámús al-muḥíṭ* (Beirut: Dár al-Jíl, 1971), vol. 3, s.v. W*D*Q. Al-Fírúzábádí

(1329–1415 A.D.) was a Persian lexicographer of Arabic born near Shiraz, who traveled widely, left Mongol-ravaged Iran and died in Yemen. He set himself to rival al-Jawharí's dictionary by producing a larger and more accurate one. He titled his work *The Encompassing Ocean.*

17. See Bahá'u'lláh, Kitáb-i-'Ahd [Book of the Covenant] in *Tablets of Bahá'u'lláh Revealed after the Kitáb-i-Aqdas,* trans. Habib Taherzadeh et al. (Haifa: Bahá'í World Centre, 1978), pp. 219–23. In this work, Bahá'u'lláh appointed his eldest son, 'Abdu'l-Bahá 'Abbás (1844–1921) to be the Center of his Covenant after his own passing. This testament was rejected by 'Abdu'l-Bahá's ambitious younger half-brother, Muḥammad-'Alí, who led a tiny band of schismatics in an ultimately unsuccessful challenge to 'Abdu'l-Bahá's authority.

18. Literally, fetishist.

19. Bahá'u'lláh, *The Kitáb-i-Íqán: The Book of Certitude* (Wilmette, Ill.: Bahá'í Publishing Trust, 1970), pp. 33–49; 61–62; 66–68.

20. Al-Ḥajjáj ibn Yúsuf (d. 714 A.D.) was the chief lieutenant of the Ummayad king 'Abdu'l-Málik (r. 692–705 A.D.). Al-Ḥajjáj reduced Mecca to obedience, bombarding the Kaaba in the process, and he ruled the eastern half of the Arab empire with an iron fist. He openly used official terrorism as a means of controlling rebellious Iraq.

21. Abú'l-Ḥasan 'Ali al-Mas'údí, *Murúj adh-dhahab wa ma'ádin al-jawhar,* with trans. C. Barbier de Meynard, vol. 5 (Paris: L'Imprimerie Imperiale, 1869), pp. 288–359 and 382–96, gives damaging anecdotes about al-Ḥajjáj, but not, apparently, this one. Al-Mas'údí (d. 956 A.D.) was an Arab historian and geographer who traveled widely and collected tales.

Khálid's father was regarded as an infidel by the devout Muslims of his day.

22. Rev. 12:4.

23. Muḥammad ash-Shahrastání (1076–1153 A.D.), author of *al-Milal wa'n-nihal* [Religious communities and creeds], was born in Khurasan. He was the principal historian of religions in medieval Islam.

24. Qur'án 19:37–39.
25. Isa. 2:4.
26. Matt. 5:5; 5:9.
27. Qur'án 28:83.
28. Gabriel Hanotaux (1853–1944) was an historian turned statesman who advocated the expansion of French colonialism. He was foreign minister from 1894 to 1898. During his time in the foreign service, French domination was firmly established in French West Africa, Madagascar, and Tunisia, and the hold on Algeria was strengthened.

The scholar referred to was Muḥammad 'Abduh (1849–1905). In his youth, 'Abduh was a radical disciple of the anti-British Pan-Islamic agitator Jamálu'd-Dín "Al-Afg͟hání" (1839–1897). 'Abduh was exiled from Egypt after the 'Urábí revolt and spent time in Europe and Beirut. In Beirut he met and became an admirer of 'Abdu'l-Bahá. Toward the end of the 1880s he gave up his earlier radicalism and returned to Egypt to work on language and education reform. In 1899 he was appointed Grand Muftí of Egypt, a post which allowed him to implement the liberal reforms of Islam he advocated. 'Abduh's reply to Hanotaux is found in *al-A'mál al-kámilah li'l-Imám Muḥammad 'Abduh* [Collected works], ed. Muḥammad 'Imarah (Beirut: Arab Institute for Studies and Publishing, 1972) 3:201–240.

29. 'Alí Yúsuf was an Egyptian intellectual who published the moderate journal *al-Mu'ayyad* in Cairo.

30. Muṣṭafá Kámil (1874–1908) was a prominent Egyptian lawyer and politician whose newspaper *al-Liwá'* [The banner] reflected his fervently nationalistic stance.

PART IV
AN ESSAY ON THE MEANING OF MIRACLES AND THE DEGREE TO WHICH EACH TYPE CONSTITUTES A PROOF

1. Matt. 12:39.
2. Matt. 16:1–4.
3. Qur'án 21:5; 20:133.

4. Qur'án 53:3–4.
5. Qur'án 8:7.
6. Reading *irháq* for *irháṣ*.
7. Qur'án 53:23.
8. *An-Naqsh fí'l-ḥajar.* Cornelius V.A. Van Dyck (1818–1895), American missionary and educator, was known for his translations from English into Arabic, a language of which he made himself complete master. He came to Beirut in 1840 and lived there the rest of his life. He became associated with the Syrian Protestant College (now the American University of Beirut). Through his translations of scientific works into Arabic, he had some influence on the development of modern Arabic prose.
9. Abú Ḥámid al-Ghazálí's *Deliverance from Error* is translated in its entirety in W. Montgomery Watt, *The Faith and Practice of al-Ghazálí* (London: George Allen and Unwin, Ltd., 1967); for this passage, see p. 22. Al-Ghazálí (1058–1111 A.D.) was born at Ṭús, Iran and studied in Baghdad. After a nervous breakdown, he forsook a brilliant career in academia to become a Sufi mystic. He went on to develop perhaps the most successful synthesis of Sunní law and theology with Sufi spirituality in medieval Islam.
10. Qur'án 13:38.
11. Qur'án 6:50.
12. Qur'án 17:90–93.
13. Averroes, *Kitáb al-kashf 'an manáhij al-adillah*, p. 221.
14. Qur'án 29:50–51.
15. Qur'án 6:50; 39:9.
16. Abú Ja'far Muḥammad al-Kulayní, *al-Uṣúl min al-káfí*, vol. 1 (Tehran: Maṭba'at al-Ḥaydarí, 1374/1955 [?]), p. 168. This is the first tradition in the section on the Proof (*al-ḥujjah*).
17. Qur'án 17:59; Deut. 6:16; Matt. 12:39.
18. Qur'án 17:59.
19. Qur'án 6:57–58.
20. Qur'án 6:109–111.
21. Qur'án 6:33–35.

22. Qur'án 8:32.
23. Qur'án 2:118.
24. Qur'án 15:12.
25. Qur'án 3:183.
26. Qur'án 10:39.
27. Qur'án 28:48–49; 13:27–28.
28. Karl Gottlieb Pfander (1803–1865) was a German pietist born in Würtemburg. He served as a missionary in India and in Transcaucasian Georgia, where he wrote *Mízán al-haqq* (Balance of truth) as a Christian polemic and apologetic work for use among Muslims in Russia. The book was published in Arabic in Cairo several times, as was a refutation of it by the Indian Muslim scholar Raḥmat Alláh. The latter's book, *Izhár al-haqq* (The demonstration of truth), was published in Cairo in 1887. Mírzá Abu'l-Faḍl may have been familiar with it.

I am indebted to Joel DeHart for the above information.

29. Qur'án 13:28.
30. Abú 'Umar 'Abd Rabbihi, *al-'Iqd al-faríd,* 7 vols., (Cairo: Maṭba'at Lajnat at-Ta'líf wa't-Tarjumah wa'n-Nashr, 1948–53) 2:239.
31. 'Alí ibn Abí Ṭálib, *Nahj al-balághah,* with notes and facing Persian trans. Ḥájj Sayyid 'Alí-Naqí Fayḍu'l-Islámí, 6 vols., (Tehran: Cháp-i Aftáb, 1326 s./1948) 3:438. This collection of discourses attributed to 'Alí was made by the Shí'í poet ash-Sharíf ar-Ráḍí (d. 1016 A.D.), and while it is so late that it probably preserves few of 'Alí's actual words, one cannot rule out the possiblity that it preserves some of his sentiments.
32. Ibn-Khaldun, *Muqaddimah,* 2:156–200. Ibn-Khaldun's rejection of Mahdism stemmed from his political and religious biases as a member of the Sunní elite in post Fáṭimid North Africa. The Ismá'ílí Shí'ís had very successfully used Mahdism to gain power in that region, and Sufi groups closer to ibn-Khaldun's own time threatened to do the same.
33. Qur'án 41:42.
34. Abú Bakr Muḥammad ibn al-Báqillání (d. 1013 A.D.)

was born in Basra and lived most of his life in Baghdad. He was a theologian of the Sunní Ash'arí school and also served as a judge and jurisprudent.

35. *Muḥiṭ al-muḥiṭ*. Buṭrus al-Bustání (1819–1883) was from a prominent Maronite family in what is now Lebanon. He converted to Protestantism and was active as a translator, journalist, lexicographer, and encyclopedist.

36. *Majma' al-baḥrayn*. Náṣíf al-Yázijí (1800–1871), from a Greek Orthodox family, was born near Beirut. His father was a physician of the school of Avicenna. He was a poet in the classical tradition and remained largely uninfluenced by European literature. He made a monumental contribution to the nineteenth-century renaissance of Arabic literature.

37. Qur'án 16:125; 3:104.

38. Qur'án 6:38; 12:111.

39. Literally, preexistent scripture. However, the "preexistence" of the Holy Book is a Sunní concept, and Abú'l-Faḍl certainly did not mean by it what the classical Sunní thinkers did. Shí'ís and Bahá'ís accept that the Holy Books are essentially originated.

40. Qur'án 8:7; 42:16.

41. Qur'án 13:2.

42. Bahá'u'lláh, *Kitáb-i-Íqán*, p. 44 ff.

43. Qur'án 28:48–49.

44. Qur'án 29:50–51.

45. Qur'án 2:1.

46. George Sale, *The Qur'an: Comprising Sale's Translation and Preliminary Discourse*, ed. E.M. Wherry (London: Kegan Paul, 1896) 1:103–5.

47. Qur'án 28:49.

48. See Rev. 11:7; cf. 'Abdu'l-Bahá, *Some Answered Questions*, p. 51.

49. The reference is to an Arabic rendering of James Murdock's translation of Johann Lorenz von Mosheim's *Institutes of Ecclesiastical History, Ancient and Modern* (New York: R. Carter and Bros., 1832). Mosheim (1694–1755) was a Lutheran scholar at Helmstadt and Göttingen, and his

history of Christianity was widely read and used in seminaries. It was criticized by some Christians for what they saw as an excessive detachment and objectivity, given that Mosheim was a Christian scholar.

50. Qur'án 69:44–47.

51. Ezek. 14:9.

52. See Ezek. 1:4–7; Jer. 1:11; Isa. 6:1–2.

53. Abú Muḥammad al-Ḥaríri (1054–1122 A.D.), Arabic poet and philologist of Basra, was famous principally for his *Maqámát* [Sessions] about a quick-witted rogue named Abú Ziyád.

Aḥmad Badí'u'z-Zamán al-Hamadání (968–1008 A.D.) was a master of both Arabic and Persian literature. He invented the genre of *maqámát*, consisting of a satire of manners in rhymed and rhythmic prose.

Abú Bakr Muḥammad al-Khwarazmí (934–993 A.D.) was an Arabic poet and writer whose fame rests largely on his epistolary style.

54. Badí'u'z-Zamán, "Wonder of the Age," was the epithet given to Aḥmad al-Hamadání.

55. Ps. 78:2 as quoted in Matt. 13:35.

56. See Dan. 12:4–9.

57. Matt. 24:30.

58. Bahá'u'lláh, *Epistle to the Son of the Wolf*, trans. Shoghi Effendi (Wilmette, Ill.: Bahá'í Publishing Trust, rev. ed. 1979), p. 53. The Mother-Book refers to the Revelation of Bahá'u'lláh.

59. Qur'án 37:173.

60. See Acts 5:12–15.

61. *Zubdat as-saḥá'if fí siyáḥat al-ma'árif.*

62. The French Revolution began in 1789. While some antireligious actions were taken earlier, the major dechristianization drive in the French Revolution came in 1793. In 1790, religious orders had been abolished. In 1793, it was decreed that bishops and parish priests be elected by the populace. In the same year, the government official Joseph Fouché forbade religious ceremonies outside the churches.

On 10 November 1793, a festival of liberty was held at Notre Dame, which was now consecrated to reason. However, Robespierre worried that a policy of militant secularism might alienate neutral foreign powers. On 6 December 1793, the Convention passed a decree reaffirming the principle of freedom of worship. The dechristianization drive of the radical government thus lost its momentum.

63. Arghún Khán (r. 1284–91): Mongol Ílkhánid ruler of Iran, who was a fanatical Buddhist. His policies were completely reversed by his successor Ghazan (1295–1304), who converted to Islam and ordered Buddhist temples in Iran destroyed and Buddhist monks driven from the realm.

Sa'du'd-Dawlah: a minister of Arghún Khán who gave control of many of Iran's districts to his Jewish relatives and attempted to eliminate Muslim influence from the Mongol government. He was eventually executed, and on his death Muslims in several cities plundered and killed Jews.

'Alá'u'd-Dín al-Khaljí (r. 1296–1316): ruler of a North Indian Muslim sultanate who imposed on all Hindus a land tax of fifty percent on each crop and strictly enforced its collection. He, like the above two examples, attempted to ensure the triumph of his religion artificially.

64. Muḥammad Báqir Majlisí (d. 1700 A.D.) was one of the greatest Shí'í divines of the Ṣafavid period in Iran. He is known for his huge compilation of traditions from the Twelve Imáms, entitled *Biḥár al-anwár* [Oceans of light].

65. Charles Loyson (1827–1912), known as Father Hyacinthe, was a prominent French Catholic dissident and reformer. After a brilliant early career in the Church, he increasingly found his conscience offended by the trend toward Roman absolutism and what he saw as an attempt to divorce the Church from the realities of nineteenth-century society. His outspoken advocacy of this position led to his excommunication in 1869. In 1879 he founded the Gallican Catholic Church, of which he became rector. This church rejected the infallibility of the Pope, advocated the election of clergy and priests by the people, replaced the

Latin liturgy with a liturgy in the national language, and allowed priests to marry. However, even this small movement grew more conservative over time, and by 1894 Father Hyacinthe had broken with it. He then devoted himself to two new efforts. The first was a political alliance of France with the Islamic world. The second was a religious alliance between the Gospel and the Qur'án. In a letter of 27 March 1895, to *L'Éclair* he wrote, "I am a Christian priest; but as a convinced disciple of Jesus Christ I do not at all believe that I do any injury to him by recognizing in Muḥammad the prophet of the Arabs." He wrote elsewhere of Muḥammad, "One cannot, without being a prophet and even a great prophet, incarnate God in the soul so profoundly, with such power and passion, and cause so many millions of men to worship Him, of all races and languages, on all continents, for fourteen centuries. . . ." (Cited in *La Grande Encyclopédie,* Paris: 1886–1902, S.V. Loyson, Charles). See also Charles Loyson, *France et Algerie: christianisme et islamisme* (Paris: E. Dentu, 1895).

66. Qur'án 40:82–83.

JUAN RICARDO COLE was born in 1952 in Albuquerque, New Mexico, where he acquired his first name from neighbors. He is of German and Scottish heritage, and his roots are in Northern Virginia. He is a doctoral candidate in Islamic Studies at the University of California, Los Angeles. He holds a Master of Arts degree in Arabic Studies from the American University of Cairo, and a Bachelor of Arts with departmental honors in the History and Literature of Religions from Northwestern University. He has published articles in academic journals on nineteenth-century Islamic intellectual history, and is writing his doctoral dissertation on Shí'í Islam in North India in the eighteenth and nineteenth centuries.

MIRACLES AND METAPHORS was designed by Anthony A. Lee; dustjacket design by Rick Kjarsgaard; composed by Freedmen's Organization, Los Angeles, in eleven on thirteen point Trump Mediaeval; printed by Kingsport Press, Kingsport, Tennessee, on sixty pound Warrens Olde Style Offset Wove; bound by Kingsport Press with Kingston natural finish with Multicolor antique end papers.